Scholars Praise
Bhagavad-gita A PHOTOGRAPHIC ESSAY

Visakha has made another unique contribution to our study of the spiritual traditions of South Asia. Her illustrated summary of the *Bhagavad-gita*, the single most influential text of Indian wisdom, comprehends and effectively communicates the timeless relevance of the *Gita* within a contemporary context. Her mature ability to blend her award-winning skills as a photographer with an appealing and convincing text are clearly in evidence here.

In this publication, we have an extraordinary opportunity to comprehend the *Gita* as it has been historically understood within its own sacred tradition, and yet at the same time grasp its message within a cutting-edge visual and literary picture of life as we live it today.

Howard J. Resnick, Ph.D. in Sanskrit and Indian Studies
from Harvard University
Visiting Scholar in Indo-European Studies, UCLA
Adjunct Professor of Sanskrit and Indian Studies,
Graduate Theological Union, Berkeley, California

Bhagavad-gita, India's most popular and widely read religious scripture, is available in nearly two thousand different versions in almost one hundred different languages. Visakha has added a further unique contribution to this illustrious ongoing commentarial heritage by blending an easy-to-read and highly accessible synopsis of the text with relevant and usefully placed photographs that highlight the essential philosophical points and make them relevant to the modern context. This version will be particularly appreciated by the non-specialized public interested in Indian spirituality.

Edwin Bryant, Ph.D.
Lecturer of Indian Studies
Harvard University

～ *Bhagavad~gita* ～

A PHOTOGRAPHIC ESSAY

By Visakha

Photomacrography: Art and Techniques (as Jean Papert)
Our Most Dear Friend: Bhagavad-gita for Children
Harmony and Bhagavad-gita:
    Lessons from a Life-Changing Move to the Wilderness

A visual guide to the world's greatest spiritual dialog

Bhagavad-gita

A PHOTOGRAPHIC ESSAY

~

A Summary Study of His Divine Grace
A. C. Bhaktivedanta Swami Prabhupada's
Bhagavad-gita As It Is

BY VISAKHA

WITH ILLUSTRATIONS BY VISAKHA AND YADUBARA

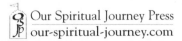
Our Spiritual Journey Press
our-spiritual-journey.com

Those who want further information on the subject matter of this book are invited to read the *Bhagavad-gita As It Is* by His Divine Grace A. C. Bhaktivedanta Swami Prabhupada, Founder-Acharya of the International Society for Krishna Consciousness. This book is available from the Bhaktivedanta Book Trust. Website: http://www.bbt.info/classics.

On the cover: "Those who perform their duty without attachment, surrendering the results to God, are unaffected by karma, as the lotus leaf is untouched by water" (*Bhagavad-gita* Chapter 5 text 10). Without God consciousness we act according to a mundane concept of our identity; with God consciousness we act knowing that our body is God's property and is best used in His service. We can then be in the world but not of the world, as a lotus leaf is in the water but not wet.

Cover design: Rasikananda Dasa.

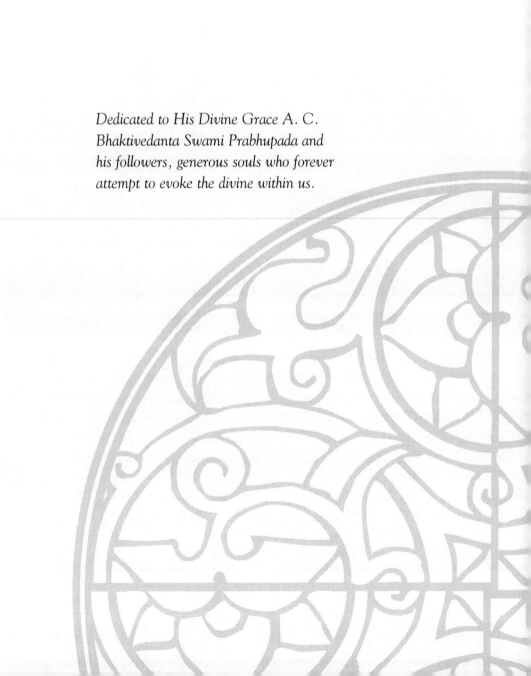

Dedicated to His Divine Grace A. C. Bhaktivedanta Swami Prabhupada and his followers, generous souls who forever attempt to evoke the divine within us.

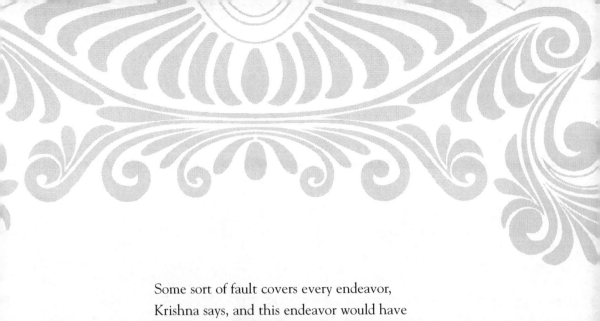

Some sort of fault covers every endeavor, Krishna says, and this endeavor would have been covered by many more faults had it not been for the clear-headed help of Jayadvaita Swami, Krishna-kripa Dasa, Devaprastha Dasa, Rasikananda Dasa, Chaitanya Daya Devi, Jai Chaitanya Dasa and Mayapriya Long, as well as my friends Bimala Devi and Lelise Folse. Also, my heartfelt gratitude to my friend and husband, Yadubara, as well as to our daughters, Rasamrita and Haripriya.

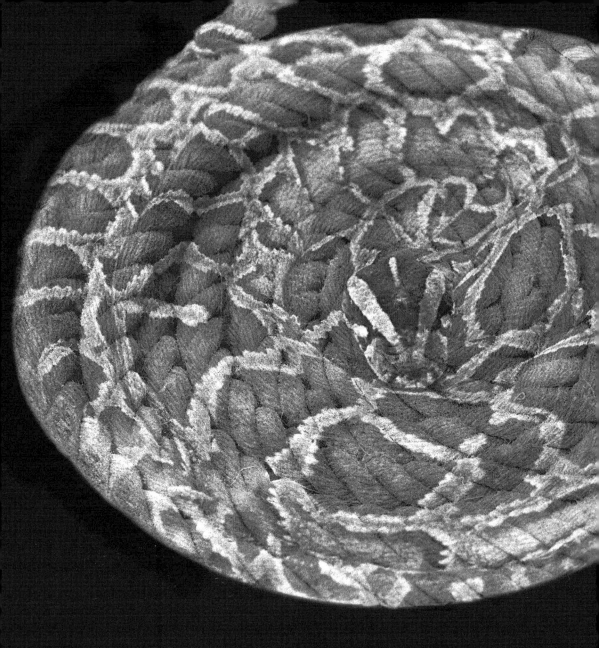

In darkness we may confuse a
rope for a snake because we
can be overcome by illusion.
Similarly, in ignorance we've
accepted our body and mind
as our self, but this is an illusion. A bona fide scripture
like the Bhagavad-gita can
free us from such an illusion.

Contents

As the opposing armies stand poised for battle, Arjuna, the
mighty warrior, sees his intimate relatives, teachers, and friends in
both armies ready to fight and sacrifice their lives. Overcome by
grief and pity, Arjuna fails in strength, his mind becomes bewildered, and he gives up his determination.

Arjuna submits to Lord Krishna as His disciple, and Krishna
begins His teachings to Arjuna by explaining the fundamental
distinction between the temporary material body and the eternal
spiritual soul. The Lord explains the process of transmigration, the
nature of selfless service to the Supreme, and the characteristics of
a self-realized person.

*The Sanskrit word "Brahman" has several meanings, namely (1) the individual soul;
(2) the impersonal, all-pervasive aspect of the Supreme; (3) the Supreme Lord; and (4)
the total material substance.

Foreword

T HE BHAGAVAD-GITA, OR GOD'S SONG, is a classical sacred text that comes to us from ancient India. Indeed, the *Bhagavad-gita* is a "song" (*gita*), as its text is found in flowing Sanskrit verse. Yet, the content of this poem takes the form of a conversation between the Supreme Lord Krishna (the *bhagavat*), and his dear friend Arjuna, who is confronted by universal existential questions that continue to challenge humans: What is my purpose in life? What should be the values by which I can make critical life decisions? What constitutes true happiness and fulfillment while in a world of moral conflict and degradation? What is the ultimate reality and what is my relationship to it? These are just some of the questions to which this text poses answers.

Often called the "Hindu" Bible, the *Bhagavad-gita* is the most loved and adored philosophical text arising from the ancient culture of South Asia. This text is a 700-verse section within the largest epic poem in the world, known as the *Mahabharata*, a magnificent epic poem at least seven times the length of both Homer's *Iliad* and *Odyssey* combined! One remarkable fact about the *Bhagavad-gita* is that it has captured the minds of and has fascinated non-Indian peoples, especially in the English-speaking world. There have been literally hundreds of translations of the text published in English alone, which is evidence that the voices from ancient India are still speaking to us in modern times.

The present work, however, is a unique presentation of key philosophical ideas and understandings of this great text. The author of this work has presented select topics and themes of the text and has explained them with the aid of photographic illustrations. Specifically, she draws from the translation and commentary of the *Bhagavad-gita* by A. C. Bhaktivedanta Swami Prabhupada (1896–1977), entitled, *Bhagavad-gita As It Is*. The reasons for this choice may be considered here. One, it may be that Prabhupada's translation and commentary, distributed by the International Society for Krishna Consciousness, is the single most widely known translation in English, as well as numerous other languages. It makes sense that the present work would focus on such a celebrated translation. Two, this translation is what I would term a "living translation" of the text, in that it is not merely the philological exercise of a specialist; rather, the Swami's work was translated clearly with the idea that it would be applied in the everyday lives of persons. Indeed, the Swami's mission was itself the cause of the worldwide spread of Vaishnava thought and practice in all major cultures of the world. Finally, the author herself, Visakha, a direct student of Bhaktivedanta Swami since 1971, has been practicing for many years the way of life that is prescribed in the *Bhagavad-gita* and in the Swami's commentary.

We are greatly benefitted by the way Visakha brings together the areas of art and religion from her own life to create the present work. The author harnesses her talents both as an accomplished writer and as a professional photographer (originally trained at the Rochester Institute of Technology). Combined with these talents are her years of dedicated practice of *bhakti-yoga*, or the practice of living a life in loving devotion to God under the guidance of this century's leading global teacher of *Bhagavad-gita*, Bhaktivedanta Swami.

The ancient, yet universally relevant message of the *Gita* is extended to us in the modern world through Visakha's clearly articulated understanding along with her powerful photographic expression of its message. I recommend this work to devotees of the religious traditions of the *Gita* and to academic students of the *Gita*, as well as to all those who desire a glimpse into the mystical vision of the *Gita*, as it is so eloquently presented herein.

Dr. Graham M. Schweig
Assistant Professor of Philosophy and Religious Studies
   Christopher Newport University

His Divine Grace A. C. Bhaktivedanta Swami Prabhupada,
author of Bhagavad-gita As It Is,
the book from which this one is derived.

Introduction

I N JUNE OF 1971 MY HUSBAND and I began a month-long trekking adventure near Pokra in Nepal. At the snow line—around 10,000 feet at that time of year—we found a small abandoned cowshed and decided to spend a few restful days. From deep inside his backpack, John, my husband, pulled out a blue paperback book with a line drawing of a regal-looking four-armed person on the cover. During our cowshed stay, I sat for hours surrounded by towering snowy peaks in crystal-clear air, with no humans other than the two of us for miles around, trying to read this early edition of *Bhagavad-gita As It Is*. Despite the pristine environs, I understood little. But I was intrigued. The idea of tolerating dualities and remaining equipoised in their midst enticed me, as did the concept of an eternal spiritual presence within all living beings and the thought of improving my character as well as the quality of my life through knowledge.

Over the intervening years, as I continued studying *Bhagavad-gita*, my respect for its wisdom, relevance, and comprehensiveness grew. In 1996 I wrote and illustrated a *Bhagavad-gita* for children, *Our Most Dear Friend* (Torchlight), and thereafter began this current version, *Bhagavad-gita: A Photographic Essay, A Visual Guide to the World's Greatest Spiritual Dialog*. This Guide does not attempt to present all 700 verses of the *Bhagavad-gita*. Rather, through the text and visuals, it presents the essential and most relevant teachings of the *Gita*, teachings that have inspired and improved my life. Thus it is called a "summary study."

Throughout the text, the speakers of the *Gita's* verses are clearly indicated, followed by the translation from Sanskrit of the verses (in quotation marks) they speak, and then by a brief commentary on those verses by A. C. Bhaktivedanta Swami Prabhupada. (On rare occasions I have incorporated part of his commentary into the verses themselves.) In this way the reader can easily follow the flow of the conversation, beginning with Arjuna's dilemma and questions, through Krishna's responses, and finally to Arjuna's ultimate realizations.

Ideas for the photographs came from both the verses of the *Gita* and the commentaries. Although some of the photographs portray the various persons involved or mentioned in the *Gita*, most illustrate philosophical points, often through analogies.

Over my years of reflection on *Bhagavad-gita*, I have found that analogies often clarify otherwise obscure philosophical concepts, vividly impress other points upon the mind, and sometimes bring a rush of understanding where previously there was none. My husband and I created some of the photographs on these pages specifically for this visual guide. Others I culled from the files we have kept on our travels as professional photojournalists.

Bhagavad-gita offers us direction that is practical, yet sublime, and it beckons us toward something mystical and delightful, to that realm which is beyond our conception. Taken from the last instructions Krishna offers to Arjuna is an example of the practical, sublime, and mystical together: "By worship of the Lord, who is the source of all beings and who is all-pervading, persons can attain perfection through performing their own work."

An Overview of the Bhagavad-gita

BHAGAVAD-GITA, A CONVERSATION between the Supreme Lord Krishna and His devotee and friend Arjuna, takes place in a dramatic setting: a battlefield on which Arjuna and his allies are poised to fight a great war. However, when Arjuna surveys the opposing army and sees his relatives prepared to conquer him or die in the attempt, he is overcome with compassion for them and unable to fight. Yet he must fight. His relatives on the opposing side have acted immorally, illegally, and dictatorially. And they've refused all offers of peaceful reconciliation.

Krishna speaks *Bhagavad-gita* to persuade Arjuna to fight, to transform his vision from the mundane to the sublime, from the material to the spiritual. And in speaking to Arjuna, He also speaks to all of us. Just as Arjuna has difficulty in fighting, so everyone has some sort of perplexity or difficulty. By His words, Krishna enables Arjuna to transcend his difficulties and reestablish his real purpose in life.

The *Bhagavad-gita* entails five basic truths: God (the Supreme Lord), the living entities, material nature, time, and the activities of the living entities (karma).

God is the supreme controller, the greatest of all. The living entities, God's parts and parcels, have His qualities in minute quantity; they are conscious and have an intimate, eternal relationship with God. Material nature, God's inferior, separated energy, is not conscious; it's constituted of three qualities: the modes of goodness, passion and ignorance. Above these modes there is time. And by a combination of these modes of nature and under the control of time, the living entities act and suffer or enjoy the results (karma).

The Supreme Lord, the living entity, material nature, and time are all interrelated and eternal. However, the other item, karma (action and reaction), is not eternal. The living entities are suffering or enjoying the results of their activities from time immemorial, but they can change their karma, and this change depends upon their knowledge.

In his introduction to the *Bhagavad-gita As It Is*, His Divine Grace A. C. Bhaktivedanta Swami Prabhupada writes, "*Bhagavad-gita* should be taken up in a spirit of devotion. One should not think that he is equal to Krishna, nor should he think that Krishna is an ordinary personality or even a very great personality. Lord Sri Krishna is the Supreme Personality of Godhead. So according to the statements of *Bhagavad-gita* or the statements of Arjuna, the person who is trying to understand the *Bhagavad-gita*, we should at least theoretically accept Sri Krishna as the Supreme Personality of Godhead, and with that submissive spirit we can understand the *Bhagavad-gita*. Unless one reads the *Bhagavad-gita* in a submissive spirit, it is very difficult to understand *Bhagavad-gita*, because it is a great mystery."

The knowledge in *Bhagavad-gita* can lead one to purify one's activities through the process of *bhakti* (loving devotional service to God). Activities in *bhakti* appear ordinary, but they are not material; they liberate one from the bodily concept of life and lead to a spirit of cooperation with the Supreme Lord. As the *Gita* ends, Arjuna accepts the path of *bhakti*.

Setting the Scene

ALTHOUGH WIDELY PUBLISHED and read by itself, *Bhagavad-gita* originally appeared as an episode in the *Mahabharata*, the epic Sanskrit history of the ancient world. The *Mahabharata* describes events leading up to the present Age of Kali. It was at the beginning of this age, some fifty centuries ago, that Lord Krishna spoke *Bhagavad-gita* to His friend and devotee Arjuna.

Their discourse—one of the most beautiful and profound texts of world literature—took place just before the onset of war, a great fratricidal conflict between the sons of Dhritarastra and their cousins, the sons of Pandu.

Dhritarastra and Pandu were brothers born into the Kuru dynasty, which descended from King Bharata, a former ruler of the earth, from whom the name *Mahabharata* derives. Because Dhritarastra, the elder brother, was born blind, the throne that otherwise would have been his went to his younger brother, Pandu.

When Pandu died at an early age, his five children—Arjuna among them—came under the care of Dhritarastra, who in effect became, for the time being, the king. Thus the sons of Dhritarastra and those of Pandu grew up in the same royal household, were trained in the military arts by the same teacher, and were counseled by the same revered "grandfather" of the clan.

Yet the sons of Dhritarastra, especially the eldest, Duryodhana, hated and envied the Pandavas (the sons of Pandu). And the blind and evil-minded Dhritarastra wanted his own sons, not those of Pandu, to inherit the kingdom.

Thus Duryodhana, with Dhritarastra's consent, plotted to kill Pandu's young sons, his cousins, and only by the careful protection of Lord Krishna did the Pandavas escape the many attempts against their lives.

Now Lord Krishna was not an ordinary man, but the Supreme Lord Himself, who had descended to earth and was playing the role of prince in a contemporary dynasty. In this role, and as the eternal upholder of religion, Krishna favored the righteous sons of Pandu.

Ultimately, however, the clever Duryodhana challenged the Pandavas to a gambling match (which was rigged), cheated them out of their kingdom, insulted their wife, and forced them into thirteen years of exile.

After their exile, the Pandavas rightfully requested the return of their kingdom from Duryodhana, who bluntly refused to yield it. Duty bound as princes to serve in public administration, the five Pandavas reduced their request to a mere five villages. But Duryodhana arrogantly replied that he wouldn't spare them even enough land into which to drive a pin. Throughout all those years, the Pandavas had been consistently tolerant and forbearing. But now war seemed inevitable.

Nonetheless, as the kings of the world divided, some siding with the sons of Dhritarastra, others with the Pandavas, Krishna Himself took the role of messenger for the sons of Pandu and went to the court of Dhritarastra to plead for peace. When His pleas were refused, war was certain.

Krishna offered to enter the war according to the desire of the antagonists. As God, He would not personally fight; but whoever so desired might have Krishna Himself as advisor and helper—and the other side, Krishna's army. The Pandavas, men of the highest moral stature, recognized Krishna as the Supreme Lord and were eager to have the Lord Himself on their side. The impious sons of Dhritarastra, however, did not recognize Krishna as the Lord and chose instead His army.

In this way, Krishna took it upon Himself to drive the chariot of the fabled bowman, Arjuna. This brings us to the point at which *Bhagavad-gita* begins, the two armies arrayed against each other, ready for combat.

~ *Bhagavad-gita* ~

A PHOTOGRAPHIC ESSAY

1

Observing the Armies on the Battlefield

AFTER LOOKING OVER THE ARMY gathered by the sons of Pandu, Duryodhana went to his teacher and said: "Behold the army of the sons of Pandu . . ." Duryodhana, the eldest of the blind king Dhritarastra's many sons, is surprised when he sees the military strength of the Pandavas (the sons of Pandu). Yet, thinking of the many heroes who had come from all parts of the world to fight on his behalf, he feels confident of victory. He asks his army to give their full support to their general, Bhisma.

Then Bhisma, the valiant general of Duryodhana's army, "blows his conchshell very loudly, making a sound like the roar of a lion, giving Duryodhana joy. After that, the conchshells, drums, bugles, trumpets, and horns all suddenly sounded, and the combined sound is tumultuous."

The sounds of these instruments enliven the soldiers to fight, and the opposing side, the Pandavas, also use them.

"On the side of the Pandavas, both Lord Krishna and Arjuna, stationed on a great chariot drawn by white horses, sound their transcendental conchshells."

King Dhritarastra

Following the lead of Krishna and Arjuna, the other great warriors on the Pandava side also blow their conchshells, and the sound becomes uproarious. "Vibrating both in the sky and on the earth, it shatters the hearts of the sons of Dhritarastra." The unexpected arrangement of military force by the Pandavas, who are guided directly by Lord Krishna, disheartens Duryodhana and his allies.

Krishna, the Supreme Lord and speaker of the Bhagavad-gita.

Arjuna addresses his chariot driver, Lord Krishna, "O infallible one, please draw my chariot between the two armies so that I may see those present here who desire to fight, and with whom I must contend in this great battle."

Lord Krishna is playing the role of Arjuna's charioteer, and because He never fails in His affection for His devotees, Arjuna addresses Him as "infallible." In all circumstances Krishna is the Supreme Lord, but in the sweetness of His transcendental relationships with His devotees, the Lord always seeks an opportunity to serve them, as they are always ready to serve Him.

"Having thus been addressed by Arjuna, Lord Krishna draws up the fine chariot in the midst of the armies of both parties and says, 'Just behold, Arjuna, all the sons of Dhritarastra and their allies assembled here.'"

On seeing his father's friends, his grandfathers, teachers, maternal uncles, cousins, the sons and grandsons of his cousins, as well as his friends and well-wishers amassed on the opposing side, Arjuna is filled with compassion.

Arjuna says,
"My dear Krishna, seeing my friends and relatives present before me in such a fighting spirit, my whole body trembles, my hair stands on end, my bow slips from my hand, and my skin burns."

Arjuna, Krishna's devotee and friend, who hears the Bhagavad-gita.

"I cannot stand here any longer. I am forgetting myself, and my mind is reeling. I see only causes of misfortune, O Krishna. I do not see how any good can come from killing my kinsmen in this battle, nor can I, my dear Krishna, desire any subsequent victory, kingdom, or happiness.

"O maintainer of all living entities, what pleasure will we derive, what should we gain, and how could we be happy by killing the sons of Dhritarastra?"

Although the sons of Dhritarastra are overtaken by greed and blind to the evil of this war, Arjuna sees the crime in destroying a family. "With the destruction of dynasty, the family tradition is vanquished, and thus the rest of the family becomes involved in irreligion.

"Alas, how strange it is that we are preparing to commit greatly sinful acts. Driven by the desire to enjoy royal happiness, we are intent on killing our own kinsmen. Better for me if the sons of Dhritarastra kill me unarmed and unresisting on the battlefield."

Arjuna is virtuous, detached, cultured, intelligent and, most importantly, devoted to God. These qualifications make him fit to receive transcendental knowledge.

Arjuna, having thus spoken on the battlefield, cast aside his bow and arrows and sat down on the chariot, his mind overwhelmed with grief.

One who hears the Bhagavad-gita as Arjuna did, accepting Krishna's message as it is, will be awakened from the confusion and frustration of daily life and drawn to the majesty of the divine. This message is clear in itself and does not require interpretation, just as the sun does not require our lamp to be visible.

A dream is terrifying until the dreamer wakes up and realizes there's nothing to fear. Similarly, Arjuna's situation is hellish until he awakens from thinking of himself as the temporary material body and sees himself as a soul, eternally existing and therefore unable to be harmed. Arjuna thus realizes that while fighting under Krishna's direction he has nothing to fear. This is the essence of Krishna's teachings in Chapter Two.

2

Contents of the Gita Summarized

S EEING ARJUNA FULL OF COMPASSION, his mind
depressed, and his eyes full of tears, Krishna begins
to enlighten Arjuna with His philosophical teachings.

The Supreme Lord
"My dear Arjuna, how have these impurities come upon
you? They are not at all befitting a person who knows the
value of life. They lead only to infamy. Give up such petty
weakness of heart and arise, O chastiser of the enemy."

Arjuna
"How can I fight with my grandfather and teacher, who
are worthy of my worship? It would be better to live by
begging than to kill them. Even though they desire
worldly gain, they are superiors. If they are killed, everything we enjoy will be tainted with blood."

Arjuna turns to Lord Krishna, the supreme spiritual
master, for a definitive solution to his perplexity. "Now I
am confused about my duty and have lost all composure
because of weakness. In this condition I am asking You to

The differences between one frame of movie film and another are so minuscule that at first glance the frames all look alike. But when the film is projected, we see the illusion of a continuous image. Similarly, though from moment to moment we transmigrate from one body to another, our different bodies are so much alike that we don't realize our own transmigration.

tell me for certain what is best for me. Now I am Your disciple, and a soul surrendered unto You. Please instruct me."

Lord Krishna smiles and replies to the grief-stricken Arjuna in the presence of both armies. *Bhagavad-gita* is not for any particular person, society, or community, but for all. Friends as well as enemies are equally entitled to hear and benefit from it.

The Supreme Lord

"While speaking learned words, you are mourning for what is not worthy of grief. Those who are wise lament neither for the living nor the dead."

The Lord immediately takes the position of a teacher and speaks strongly, indirectly telling Arjuna that he's a fool. A learned person knows that the body will die eventually; therefore the body is not as important as the soul. One who knows this does not lament, regardless of the condition of the body.

"Never was there a time when I did not exist, nor you, nor all these kings; nor in the future shall any of us cease to be."

The Lord says that He Himself, Arjuna, and all the fighters are eternally individual spiritual beings. They existed as spiritual individuals in the past, and they will remain eternal spiritual persons. Their individuality existed in the past and will continue in the future.

The soul does not age as the body does. The so-called old man may therefore keep his youthful spirit although his body can't work as well as it did when young.

Therefore, there is no cause for lamentation for anyone. The Lord then gives evidence of the soul's existence in the body and explains what happens to it after it leaves this body.

"As the embodied soul continuously passes, in this body, from childhood to youth to old age, the soul similarly

As winter comes and goes, so do happiness and distress. Krishna tells Arjuna to remain even-minded though perceiving such dualities. As a man must do his work in spite of bad weather, or a student must go to school even though he would rather not, Arjuna must fight because it's his duty as a soldier. He should not forsake his duty because of the temporary pains that arise in the course of its performance.

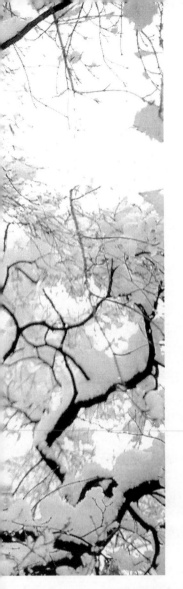

passes into another body at death. A sober person is not bewildered by such a change. As a person puts on new garments, giving up old ones, the soul similarly accepts new material bodies, giving up the old and useless ones."

Since every living entity is an individual soul, each is changing its body at every moment, manifesting sometimes as a child, sometimes as a youth, and sometimes as an old person. Yet the same spirit soul dwells within and does not undergo any change. At death this individual soul leaves the body and transmigrates to another body, as one gives up an old coat for a new one.

As long as one has a material body, one sometimes experiences happiness and at other times misery, much as one experiences alternating summer and winter seasons. Krishna advises Arjuna to tolerate these fluctuations without being disturbed, for one who does so is eligible for liberation. He then explains the nature of the soul.

Lord Krishna continues,
"Those who are seers of the truth have concluded that the material body does not endure and the soul does not change."

The body is changing at every moment by the action and reaction of the different cells, and thus growth and old age take place. But the spirit soul exists eternally, remaining despite all mental and bodily changes.

The symptom of the soul's presence is consciousness. Each person is conscious of the pleasures and pains of his or her body, and therefore each body is the embodiment of an individual soul. This soul is a spiritual atom, smaller than the material atoms. Such atoms are innumerable and cannot be perceived by material instruments.

A spirit soul dwells in the heart of each living entity, and thus all the energies of bodily movement emanate from the heart. The corpuscles that carry oxygen from the lungs gather energy from the soul. When the soul leaves the body, the activity of the blood ceases. The material body minus consciousness is a dead body, and this consciousness cannot be revived in the body by any material means. Medical science accepts the importance of the red corpuscles, but it cannot ascertain that the source of the energy is the soul, although medical science does admit that the heart is the seat of all energies of the body.

"The soul pervades the entire body and is indestructible. No one is able to destroy the imperishable soul. For the soul there is neither birth nor death at any time. It is unborn, eternal, ever-existing, and primeval. It is not slain when the body is slain. The soul can never be cut to pieces by any weapon, nor burned by fire, nor moistened by water, nor withered by the wind. This individual soul is unbreakable and insoluble."

Then the Lord begins speaking of Arjuna's duty. Since Arjuna is a military man, the best engagement for him is to fight for religious principles; and so he need not hesitate. His duty is to protect the citizens from all kinds of difficulties, and for that reason he is obliged to apply violence in this case to maintain law and order. "If you do not perform your religious duty of fighting," Krishna says,

"then you will certainly incur sins for neglecting your duties and thus lose your reputation as a fighter.

"Fight for the sake of fighting, without considering happiness or distress, loss or gain, victory or defeat—and by so doing you shall never incur sin."

Arjuna thinks that he will receive sinful reactions by fighting, but Lord Krishna explains why that isn't so.

"Now listen as I explain how to work without fruitive results. When you act in such knowledge, you can free yourself from the bondage of works.

"You have a right to perform your prescribed duty, but you are not entitled to the fruits of action. Never consider yourself the cause of the results of your activities, and never be attached to not doing your duty."

The Lord advises Arjuna not to

Even from the materialistic viewpoint, Arjuna had no reason to lament. When the body—or a building, or any form of matter—is destroyed, it becomes unmanifest and remains ultimately as atoms. In course of time things are manifested and then unmanifested, and in either stage nothing is lost. So what cause is there for lamentation?

be inactive, but to perform his duty without being attached to the result. Attachment means accepting things for one's own sense gratification, and detachment is the absence of such sensual attachment. But those fixed in Krishna consciousness have neither attachment nor detachment because their lives are dedicated to the service of the Lord. One who is attached to the result of one's work is also bound to the reaction: either enjoyment or suffering. Arjuna's nonparticipation in the battle is another side of attachment; and any attachment, positive or negative, is cause for bondage. Inaction is sinful. Therefore, fighting as a matter of duty under the direction of the Lord is the only auspicious path for Arjuna.

"Perform your duty equipoised, O Arjuna, abandoning all attachment to success or failure. Such equanimity is called yoga."

Yoga means to concentrate the mind upon the Supreme Lord by controlling the ever-disturbing senses, and to follow His directions. In the highest sense, "yoga" means to link with the Supreme Lord by pleasing Him with loving devotional service.

"Persons engaged in devotional service rid themselves of both good and bad actions, even in this life. Therefore strive for yoga, which is the art of all work."

By engaging in devotional service to the Lord, great devotees have freed themselves from the results of work in the material world, and thus from the cycle of birth and death. Lord Krishna encourages Arjuna to follow their example and attain that state beyond all miseries, the spiritual kingdom. If he tries in this way, he will never be the loser.

"In this endeavor there is no loss or diminution, and a little advancement on this path can protect one from the most dangerous type of fear." Unlike material activities and their results, which end with the body, God conscious activities have a permanent effect. If a person completes two percent in Krishna consciousness in this lifetime, the next beginning will be from three percent.

One who is able to withdraw one's senses from sense objects, as the tortoise draws its limbs within the shell, is firmly fixed in perfect consciousness.

*As a strong wind
sweeps away a boat
on the water, even
one of the roaming
senses on which
the mind focuses can
carry away a person's
intelligence.*

Though one may be restricted from sense enjoyment, one's taste for sense objects remains. But by experiencing a higher taste, the taste of serving the Lord with love, one stops seeking sense enjoyment and becomes fixed in God consciousness. On the path of God consciousness, however, there may be obstacles.

"The senses are so strong and impetuous, O Arjuna, that they forcibly carry away the mind even of a person of discrimination who is endeavoring to control them."

By contemplating sense objects, one develops attachment for them, and from such attachment lust develops, and when lust is unfulfilled, anger follows.

But those who are free from attachment and aversion, who control the senses and fix their consciousness upon the Lord, can receive His mercy. One who is not connected with the Supreme, however, can have neither transcendental intelligence nor a steady mind, without which there is no possibility of peace. "And," Krishna asks Arjuna, "how can there be any happiness without peace?"

It's not that the Lord expects Arjuna to become free of material demands—as long as one has a material body, the demands of the body for sense gratification will continue. But He does expect Arjuna to be undisturbed by material desires, for even one of the senses engaged in the desire for material pleasure can create a disturbance.

The Supreme Lord concludes,
"A person who is not disturbed by the incessant flow of desires—that enter like rivers into the ocean, which is ever being filled but is always still—can alone achieve peace, and not the person who strives to satisfy such desires.

"That is the way of the spiritual and godly life, after which attained, a person is not bewildered. If one is thus situated, even at the hour of death, one can enter into the kingdom of God."

Desires are compared to rivers, and the ocean is compared to a saintly person's mind. Although many turbulent rivers fill the ocean with their waters, the ocean remains undisturbed. Similarly, although desires may come upon saintly persons, such persons are not disturbed, for they are full in themselves. Thus they remain peaceful.

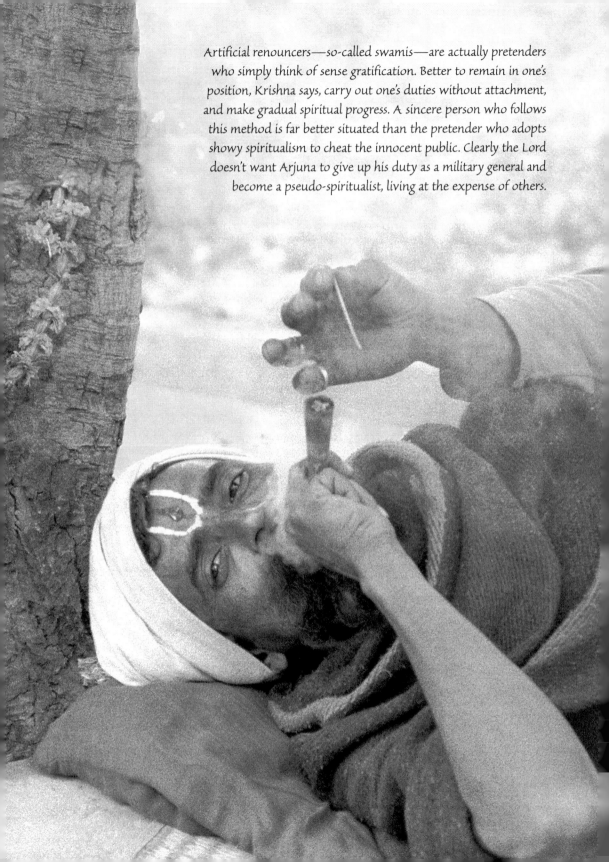

Artificial renouncers—so-called swamis—are actually pretenders who simply think of sense gratification. Better to remain in one's position, Krishna says, carry out one's duties without attachment, and make gradual spiritual progress. A sincere person who follows this method is far better situated than the pretender who adopts showy spiritualism to cheat the innocent public. Clearly the Lord doesn't want Arjuna to give up his duty as a military general and become a pseudo-spiritualist, living at the expense of others.

3

Karma-yoga

ARJUNA IS CONFUSED. Krishna has told him to control his senses and become detached, perhaps indicating that Krishna consciousness means inaction. Yet the Lord also said that Arjuna should fight. As a sincere student, Arjuna asks for clarification.

Arjuna
"O Krishna, why do You want to engage me in this ghastly warfare, if You think that intelligence is better than fruitive work?"

One cannot even maintain one's physical body without work. But work done for sense gratification has a reaction, either good or bad, and any reaction binds the performer. "Therefore, O Arjuna," Krishna says, "perform your prescribed duties for My satisfaction, and in that way always remain free from bondage."

To attain this exalted stage, Arjuna should act as a matter of duty, without being attached to the fruits of his activities; he should fight in the battle for the interest of

In a living
form,
a soul is
present;
in a
lifeless
one, it
isn't.

All the necessities of life—food, water, air, light—are supplied not by factories but by material nature which works under the direction of the Supreme Lord. If there's no rain, then despite all our technological advancement, crops die.

Krishna because Krishna wants him to fight. Arjuna's idea to be a good or non-violent man is a personal attachment, but for him to act on behalf of the Supreme is to act without attachment to the result. That is perfect action, recommended by the Supreme Lord Krishna, and it is transcendental to all reactions.

"Whatever action a great person performs, common people follow. And whatever standards that person sets by exemplary acts, all the world pursues.

"As the ignorant perform their duties with attachment to results, the learned person may similarly act, but without attachment, for the sake of leading people on the right path.

"Therefore, O Arjuna, surrendering all your works unto Me, with full knowledge of Me, without desires for profit, with no claims to proprietorship, and free from lethargy, fight."

The cashier counts millions of dollars for her employer but claims not a cent for herself. Similarly, one who sees everything in relation to God realizes that everything belongs to Him.

Krishna has several times asked Arjuna to be dutiful and detached, but here for the first time He asks Arjuna to fight with devotion. He then describes the result of acting in this way.

"Persons who execute their duties according to My injunctions and who follow this teaching faithfully, without envy, become free from the bondage of fruitive actions. But those who, out of envy, disregard these teachings and do not follow them are bereft of all knowledge, befooled, and ruined in their endeavors for perfection."

The simple qualification of firm faith in the eternal injunctions of the Lord, even by a beginner who's unable to execute such injunctions, qualifies one to become liberated from karma. In the beginning of Krishna consciousness, one may not fully discharge the injunctions of the Lord, but because one is not resentful of this principle and works sincerely, without consideration of defeat and hopelessness, one will surely be promoted to the stage of pure Krishna consciousness. Krishna doesn't want Arjuna to give up his duties abruptly, but to remain in his position and try to become God conscious. In this way he will gradually become detached from all kinds of sensual activities.

Arjuna
"O Krishna, by what is one impelled to sinful acts, even unwillingly, as if engaged by force?"

The Supreme Lord
"It is lust only, Arjuna, which is born of contact with the material mode of passion and later transformed into wrath, and which is the all-devouring sinful enemy of this world. The wise living entity's pure consciousness becomes covered by its eternal enemy in the form of lust, which is never satisfied and which burns like fire." When living entities come in contact with the material creation, their eternal love for Krishna is transformed into lust. When lust is unsatisfied, it turns into wrath; wrath is transformed into illusion, and illusion continues the material existence. Therefore, lust is the greatest enemy of the living

entity, and it is lust only that induces the pure living entity to remain entangled in this material world.

"The senses, mind, and intelligence are the sitting places of this lust. Through these, lust covers the real knowledge of the living entities and bewilders them. Therefore, in the very beginning curb this great symbol of sin, lust, by regulating the senses, and slay this destroyer of knowledge and self-realization." When love of God deteriorates into lust, it's very difficult to return to the normal, God conscious condition; but it is possible by devotional service to the Supreme Lord, in which the soul is directly engaged with the Supreme. Then the soul's subordinates — the intelligence, mind, and senses — will be similarly engaged.

"Thus knowing oneself to be transcendental to the material senses, mind, and intelligence, O mighty-armed Arjuna, one should steady the mind by deliberate spiritual intelligence and thus—by spiritual strength—conquer this insatiable enemy known as lust." If lust is transformed into love for the Supreme, or transformed into Krishna consciousness—in other words, desiring everything for Krishna—then lust can be spiritualized and thus conquered.

In summary, Arjuna's desire for sense gratification is his greatest enemy, but by dedicating his work to Krishna (*karma-yoga*), he could control his senses, mind, and intelligence and thus gradually become transcendentally situated.

As one who breaks the law is imprisoned, the soul covered by lust is imprisoned in the material world.

Ignorance is
compared to a
dangerous body
of water, and
transcendental
knowledge to
the boat that
can safely carry
one across it.

4

Transcendental Knowledge

AFTER RECOMMENDING KARMA-YOGA (non-fruitive action), Krishna explains how this yoga culminates in transcendental knowledge—knowledge concerning God, the soul, and their eternal relationship.

Krishna first mentions the history of the oral transmission of the *Gita* (originating with Himself) through disciplic succession.

The Supreme Lord
"I instructed this imperishable science of yoga to the sun-god, Vivasvan, and Vivasvan instructed it to Manu, the father of mankind, and Manu in turn instructed it to Iksvaku. This supreme science was thus received through the chain of disciplic succession, and the saintly kings understood it in that way. But in course of time the succession was broken, and therefore the science as it is appears to be lost."

When unscrupulous commentators interpret the *Gita* to accommodate their own interests, they distort the original purpose of this great text and cover its eternal truths.

Lord Krishna manifested Himself as Lord Buddha (below), and also as Lord Chaitanya (right). As Lord Chaitanya He propagated a sublime and easy method of God realization especially suited for this age of quarrel, namely the chanting of the Lord's holy names: Hare Krishna, Hare Krishna, Krishna Krishna Hare Hare/Hare Rama, Hare Rama, Rama Rama, Hare Hare.

Krishna is speaking it again to reestablish those truths.

"That very ancient science of the relationship with the Supreme is today told by Me to you because you are My devotee as well as My friend and can therefore understand the transcendental mystery of this science."

After assuring Arjuna that he is qualified to receive this knowledge, Krishna explains His transcendental nature as the Supreme Lord and the reason for His periodic descents to the material world.

"Although I am unborn and My transcendental body never deteriorates, and although I am the Lord of all living entities, I still appear in every millennium in My original transcendental form."

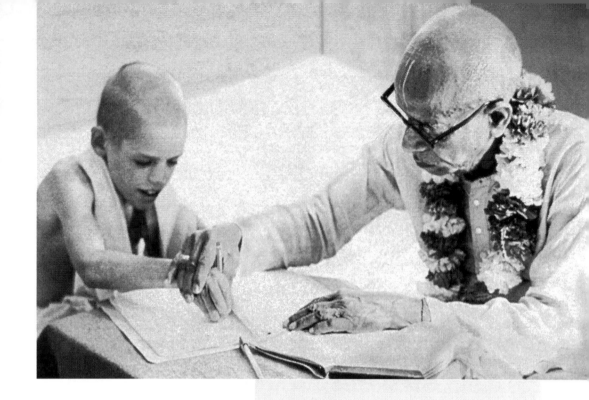

As a teacher instructs a student, one who is mature in spiritual realization teaches a neophyte. In this way—from a qualified spiritual teacher to a qualified spiritual student—the science of God consciousness has been passed down through the ages.

The Lord's appearance and disappearance is like the sun's rising, moving before us, and then disappearing from our sight. When the sun is out of sight, we think that the sun is set, and when the sun is before our eyes, we think that the sun is on the horizon. Actually, the sun is always in its fixed position, but owing to our defective, insufficient senses, we calculate the appearance and disappearance of the sun.

Unlike the living entities in the material world, the Lord does not transmigrate from one body to another.

Whenever He appears, He does so in the same original spiritual body, which never grows old or deteriorates. The Lord is conscious of all His previous appearances and disappearances, while the living entities forget everything about their past body as soon as they enter another body.

"Whenever and wherever there is a decline in religious practice, O Arjuna, and a predominant rise of irreligion—at that time I descend Myself. To deliver the pious and to annihilate the miscreants, as well as to reestablish the principles of religion, I Myself appear, millennium after millennium." Although there are many transcendental forms of the Lord, they are still the same Supreme Person. Each incarnation of the Lord has a particular mission, which is described in the revealed scriptures. No one should be accepted as an incarnation unless the scriptures refer to him. The Lord's mission is always the same: to lead people to God consciousness and obedience to the principles of religion. Sometimes He descends personally, and sometimes He sends His bona fide representative in the form of His son, or servant, or Himself in some disguised form.

"Those who know the transcendental nature of My appearance and activities do not, upon leaving the body, take their birth again in this material world, but attain My eternal abode, O Arjuna.

"Being freed from attachment, fear and anger, being fully absorbed in Me and taking refuge in Me, many, many persons in the past became purified by knowledge of Me—and thus they all attained transcendental love for Me." Some people are too materially attached and therefore do not give attention to spiritual life, some are fearful of

The blazing fire of life's perplexities and anxieties can be extinguished by hearing from a qualified spiritual teacher.

spiritual individuality and personality and want to merge into the supreme spirit, and some disbelieve in everything, being angry at all sorts of spiritual speculation out of hopelessness. For success in spiritual life, one must rid oneself of attachment to, fear of, and anger about the material world by the process of devotional service.

"As all surrender unto Me, I reward them accordingly. Everyone follows My path in all respects, O Arjuna."

Everyone is dependent for success upon God's mercy alone, and all kinds of spiritual processes are but different degrees of success on the same path. Whether one is without material desires, or full of material desires, or seeks liberation, one should with all effort worship the Supreme Lord for complete perfection, culminating in God consciousness.

Most people, however, have little interest in spiritual knowledge. Rather, they work hard for material enjoyment through the pursuit of wealth, power, and prestige. Recognizing these prevalent tendencies, Lord Krishna created a social system so that everyone, while working according to their propensity, could also make spiritual advancement.

"Just try to learn the truth by approaching a spiritual master," Lord Krishna says. "Inquire submissively and render service unto such a person. The self-realized souls can impart knowledge unto you because they have seen the truth."

No one can be spiritually realized by manufacturing a process; mental speculation and dry arguments cannot lead one to the right path. Nor by independent study of books of knowledge can one progress in spiritual life. One must approach a bona fide spiritual master in the line of disciplic succession from the Lord Himself, and accept and serve such a highly qualified spiritual master without false prestige. Satisfaction of the self-realized spiritual master is the secret of advancement in spiritual life.

"Having obtained real knowledge from a self-realized soul, you will never fall again into such illusion, for by this knowledge you will see that all living beings are but part of the Supreme, or in other words, that they are Mine." Arjuna, under illusion, thought that the temporary bodily relationship with his kinsmen was more important than his eternal spiritual relationship with Krishna, but in reality his kinsmen are Krishna's eternal servitors, as is Arjuna himself. Having forgotten his eternal service, Arjuna is perplexed by the material energy.

"Even if you are considered to be the most sinful of all sinners, when you are situated in the boat of transcendental knowledge you will be able to cross over the ocean of miseries." In the ocean, however expert a swimmer one may be, the struggle for existence is severe. If someone

The science of self-realization is the boat that enables one to cross the ocean of miseries.

comes and lifts the struggling swimmer from the ocean, that person is the greatest savior.

"As blazing fire turns firewood to ashes, O Arjuna, so does the fire of knowledge burn to ashes all reactions to material activities. In this world, there is nothing so sublime and pure as transcendental knowledge. Such knowledge is the mature fruit of all mysticism. And those who have become accomplished in the practice of devotional service enjoy this knowledge within themselves in due course of time.

"Faithful persons who are dedicated to transcendental knowledge and who subdue their senses are eligible to achieve such knowledge, and having achieved it they quickly attain the supreme spiritual peace. But ignorant and faithless persons who doubt the revealed scriptures do

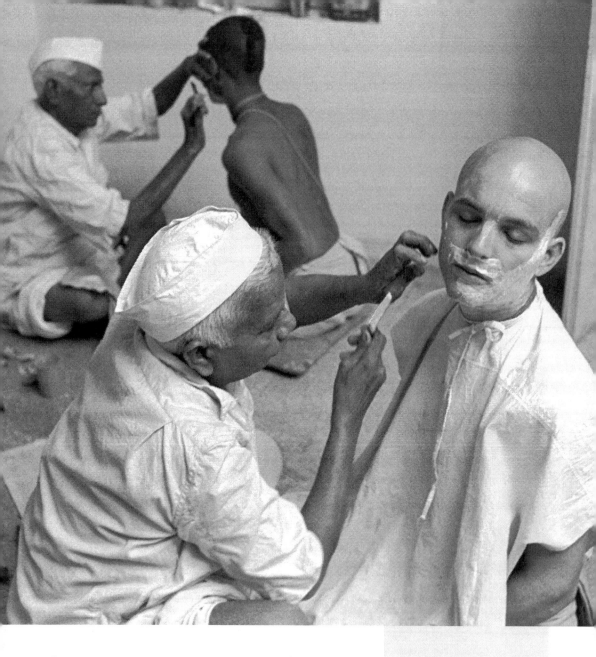

Even in ordinary dealings, faith is required—you must have faith that the barber won't slit your throat with his blade. Similarly, in spiritual life, faith in the bona fide teachers and scriptures is required.

not attain God consciousness; they fall down. For the doubting soul there is happiness neither in this world nor in the next.

"Therefore the doubts which have arisen in your heart out of ignorance should be slashed by the weapon of knowledge. Armed with yoga, O Arjuna, stand and fight."

A person situated in the self sees that the soul within, not the body, is the attractive, joyful, loving force. When the soul leaves the body (at death), the body is no longer attractive.

5

Action in Krishna Consciousness

IN CHAPTER THREE, KRISHNA SAYS that one who is self-realized has no duties. Yet at the end of Chapter Four, Krishna tells Arjuna to arm himself with yoga and fight. Arjuna wonders if he should be inactive in knowledge or active in devotion.

Arjuna
"O Krishna, first of all You ask me to renounce work, and then again You recommend work with devotion. Now will You kindly tell me definitely which of the two is more beneficial?"

The Supreme Lord
"The renunciation of work and work in devotion are both good for liberation. But, of the two, work in devotional service is better than renunciation of work." Renunciation is complete when done with the knowledge that everything in existence belongs to the Lord. One should understand that, factually, since nothing belongs

When from a distance we watch a person fly a kite, we can't always tell if she's letting the kite go higher or bringing it down. Nor from what people are doing can we always tell if they are becoming free from karma or taking on more.

to anyone, then where is the question of proprietorship or of renunciation? One who knows that everything is Krishna's property is always situated in renunciation. Since everything belongs to Krishna, we should employ everything in His service.

"Those who perform their duty without attachment, surrendering the results unto the Supreme Lord, are unaffected by sinful action, as lotus leaves are untouched by water." Even our material body, being a gift of the Lord for carrying out a particular type of action, can be engaged in Krishna consciousness. Then our body becomes uncontaminated by sinful reactions, exactly as the lotus leaf, though in a pond, is not wet.

"The steadily devoted souls attain unadulterated peace because they offer the result of all activities to Me; whereas persons who are not in union with the Divine, who are greedy for the fruits of their labor, become entangled."

When we are bewildered by material desires, the Lord allows us to fulfill those desires, but the Lord is never responsible for the actions and reactions that result from those desires. The Lord can fulfill all desires, but, being neutral to everyone, He does not interfere with our desires. However, when we desire Him, the Lord takes special care and encourages us to desire in such a way that we can attain Him and be eternally happy.

"When one is enlightened with the knowledge by which ignorance is destroyed, then one's knowledge reveals everything, as the sun lights up everything in the daytime."

A wise person is in the world but not of it, as the lotus leaf is in the water but not wet.

An enlightened person distinguishes neither between species nor castes. In Krishna's words, "The humble sages, by virtue of true knowledge, see with equal vision a learned and gentle *brahmana*, a cow, an elephant, a dog, and a dog-eater." The *brahmana* (learned, pious teacher) and the dog-eater may differ from the social point of view, or a dog, a cow, and an elephant may differ from the point of view of species, but these bodily distinctions are meaningless from the transcendentalist's viewpoint. This equanimity of vision is the sign of self-realization. As the Lord is flawless, being free from attraction or hatred, so when living entities relinquish attraction or hatred, they also become flawless and eligible to enter God's kingdom. Such persons know perfectly well that they are not their bodies, but fragmental portions of the Supreme Lord. Many transcendental symptoms result from this realization.

"A person who neither rejoices upon achieving something pleasant nor laments upon obtaining something unpleasant, who is self-intelligent, who is unbewildered, and who knows the science of God, is already situated in transcendence. Such a liberated person is not attracted to material sense

Within each living thing a soul resides, equal in quality to all others. Spiritually, all living beings are equal.

pleasure but is always in trance, enjoying the pleasure within. In this way the self-realized person enjoys unlimited happiness by concentrating on the Supreme.

"An intelligent person does not take part in the sources of misery, which are due to contact with the material senses. O Arjuna, such pleasures have a beginning and an end, and so the wise person does not delight in them.

"Before giving up this present body, if one is able to tolerate the urges of the material senses and check the force of desire and anger, one is well situated and is happy in this world. One whose happiness is within, who is active and rejoices within, and whose aim is inward is actually the perfect mystic. Such a person is liberated by experiencing the Supreme within, and thereby ultimately attains the Supreme."

In Krishna's view, welfare work does not mean only ministering to the physical welfare of human society. Temporary relief for the body is incomplete. The cause of difficulties in life is forgetfulness of our relationship with the Supreme Lord. So true welfare work must also include reviving our God consciousness and the God consciousness within other living beings.

When friends wear costumes, they are unrecognizable. Similarly, every soul in this world is dressed with a material body and cannot be recognized by material vision.

"A person in full consciousness of Me, knowing Me as the ultimate enjoyer of all sacrifices and austerities, the Supreme Lord of all planets and demigods, and the benefactor and well-wisher of all living entities, attains peace from the pangs of material miseries." People are anxious about attaining peace in the material world. But they do not know the formula for peace, which Krishna explains in this part of the *Bhagavad-gita*. The greatest peace formula is simply this: whatever work we do is meant to be offered unto God. We should do everything for and offer everything to the transcendental service of the Lord because He is the proprietor of everything. No one is greater than He, and He is the greatest friend of each living being.

Under the spell of illusion, living entities are trying to be lords of the material energy, but actually they are dominated by it. Krishna is the master of material nature, and the conditioned souls are under the stringent rules of material nature. Those who understand these facts will achieve peace in the world, individually and collectively. Krishna consciousness brings one into spiritual life even while one is within the jurisdiction of matter, for its practice arouses spiritual existence in the material world. And it can award peace to the human being.

A hired carpenter cannot rightly claim that his creations are his; they belong to his employer. In the same way, whatever we have and whatever we create belong to God, for He has provided all the natural resources we utilize, as well as our ability and intelligence to utilize them.

6

The Yoga of Meditation

IN THIS CHAPTER THE LORD EXPLAINS a process of yoga for controlling the mind and senses, and He explains that the perfect yogi is the person who acts for the satisfaction of the Supreme.

The Supreme Lord
"A person is said to be elevated in yoga when, having renounced all material desires, that person neither acts for sense gratification nor engages in fruitive activities.

"We must deliver ourselves with the help of our minds, and not degrade ourselves. The mind is the friend of the conditioned soul, and the enemy as well. For one who has conquered the mind, the mind is the best of friends; but for one who has failed to do so, the mind will remain the greatest enemy."

One who cannot control the mind lives always with the greatest enemy, and thus one's life and its mission are spoiled. As long as the mind remains an unconquered enemy, one has to serve the dictates of lust, greed, hatred,

A wild, unbridled horse is like an uncontrolled mind—unpredictable, disturbing, and dangerous. In this chapter Krishna explains the importance of conquering the mind, gives the means for doing so, and speaks of the resulting self-mastery.

envy, and anger. But when the mind is conquered, one voluntarily agrees to abide by the dictations of the Supreme Lord, who is situated within everyone's heart as the Supersoul. "For those who have conquered the mind, the Supersoul is already reached, for they are tranquil. To such people, happiness and distress, heat and cold, honor and dishonor are all the same.

"One is said to be established in self-realization and is called a yogi when one is fully satisfied by virtue of acquired knowledge and realization. Such a person is situated in transcendence, is self-controlled, and sees everything—whether it be pebbles, stones, or gold—as the same.

"One is considered still further advanced when one regards honest well-wishers, affectionate benefactors, the neutral, mediators, the envious, friends and enemies, the pious and the sinners all with an equal mind.

"To practice yoga, one should go to a secluded place and should lay kusa grass on the ground and then cover it with a deerskin and a soft cloth. The seat should be neither too high nor too low and should be situated in a sacred place. The yogi should then sit on it firmly and practice yoga to purify the heart

Out of many good medicines, a doctor prescribes the one that's right for us. Similarly, out of many bona fide ways of self-realization—one being the mystic yoga process mentioned above—Krishna prescribes the way that's best for us. He's the expert doctor and at the end of this chapter He gives us His personal advice.

by controlling the mind, senses, and activities, and fixing the mind on one point. One should hold one's body, neck, and head erect in a straight line and stare steadily at the tip of the nose. Thus, with an unagitated, subdued mind, devoid of fear, completely free from sex life, one should meditate upon Me within the heart and make Me the ultimate goal of life." This process of spiritual realization, suitable for previous ages, is often not possible to follow in this age of quarrel and hypocrisy. As the Lord will later explain, we can attain the same goal by the process of *bhakti-yoga.*

"There is no possibility of one's becoming a yogi, O Arjuna, if one eats too much or eats too little, sleeps too much or does not sleep enough. One who is regulated in the habits of eating, sleeping, recreation, and work can mitigate all material pains by practicing the yoga system.

"In the stage of perfection called trance, or *samadhi*, one's mind is completely restrained from material mental activities by practice of yoga. This perfection is characterized by one's ability to see the soul and the Supersoul (God in the heart of all living beings) by the pure mind and to relish and rejoice in the Supersoul. In that joyous state, one is situated in boundless transcendental happiness, realized through transcendental senses. Thus established, one never departs from the truth, and upon gaining this position one thinks

As a flame in a windless place does not waver, so the transcendentalist, whose mind is controlled, remains always steady in meditation on the transcendent Self.

there is no greater gain. Being thus situated, one is never shaken, even in the midst of greatest difficulty. This indeed is actual freedom from all miseries arising from material contact.

"From wherever the mind wanders due to its flickering and unsteady nature, one must certainly withdraw it and bring it back under the control of the self."

Arjuna
"O Krishna, the system of yoga which You have summarized appears impractical and unendurable to me, for the mind is restless, unsteady, turbulent, obstinate, and very strong, O Krishna, and to subdue it, I think, is more difficult than controlling the wind." Arjuna rejects as impractical the system of mysticism described by Lord Krishna. In this age most people cannot leave home for a secluded place in the mountains or jungle to practice yoga. People are not concerned about self-realization even by simple means, what to speak of such a difficult yoga system. As a practical man, Arjuna thought it impossible to practice this system of yoga, even though he belonged to the royal family, was an accomplished fighter, had great longevity, and, above all, was the most intimate friend of Lord Krishna, the Supreme Person. Therefore, if impossible for Arjuna, how could this system apply to the ordinary person?

Lord Krishna
"O mighty-armed one, it is undoubtedly very difficult to curb the restless mind, but it is possible by suitable

practice and by detachment." The foremost "suitable practice" is to hear about God. The more one hears about God, the more one becomes enlightened and detached from everything that draws the mind away from God. "Hearing" includes not only learning from self-realized souls, but also studying and contemplating God's words in authorized scriptures like the *Bhagavad-gita*. Thus reading the *Bhagavad-gita* is also a "suitable practice."

"For one whose mind is unbridled, self-realization is difficult work. But one whose mind is controlled and who strives by appropriate means is assured of success. That is My opinion." Trying to practice yoga while engaging the mind in material enjoyment is like trying to ignite a fire while pouring water on it. Such a show of yoga may be materially lucrative, but it is useless as far as spiritual realization is concerned.

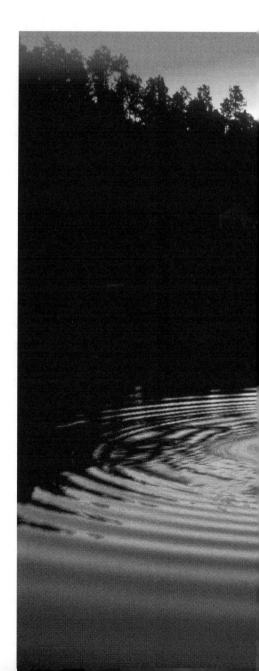

Like the mind, water is easily disturbed. But when water is sheltered it gradually becomes calm, like the mind that follows the regulations of yoga.

Arjuna

"O Krishna, what is the destination of the unsuccessful transcendentalist, who in the beginning takes to the process of self-realization with faith, but who later desists due to worldly-mindedness and thus does not attain perfection in mysticism?

"O Krishna, does not such a person, who is bewildered from the path of transcendence, fall away from both spiritual and material success and perish like a riven cloud, with no position in any sphere? This is my doubt, O Krishna, and I ask You to dispel it completely." Despite endeavoring for self-realization, one may fail if one is not sufficiently serious about following the process. To pursue the transcendental path is an attempt to escape the clutches of material vision—to declare war against it. So the material energy tries to defeat the practitioner by various allurements. A conditioned soul identifies itself with the material body and so is already allured by the material energy. And there is every chance of it being allured again, even while performing transcendental disciplines.

The Supreme Lord

"Arjuna, a transcendentalist engaged in auspicious activities does not meet with destruction either in this world or in the spiritual world; one who does good, My friend, is never overcome by evil. Yogis who are unsuccessful after a short practice of yoga enjoy many years on higher planets (where pious living entities reside), and then are reborn on this planet into a family of righteous people or a family

Arjuna compares the churning, strong, obstinate mind to the wind. As the wind cannot be stopped, neither can the mind. But Krishna explains that by suitable practice—hearing about the Lord—and by detachment from material life, the mind can be controlled.

of rich aristocracy. However, if unsuccessful after a long
practice of yoga, they take birth in a family of transcen-
dentalists who are surely great in wisdom. Certainly, such
a birth is rare in this world.

"On taking such a birth, those persons revive the
divine consciousness of their previous lives, and again
try to make further progress in order to achieve complete

success. By virtue of their divine consciousness of the previous life, they automatically become attracted to the
yogic principles—even without seeking them. And when
a yogi engages with sincere endeavor in making further
progress, being washed of all contaminations, then ultimately, achieving perfection after many, many births of
practice, that person attains the supreme goal.

"A yogi is greater than the ascetic, greater than the empiricist, and greater than the fruitive worker. Therefore, O Arjuna, in all circumstances, be a yogi. And of all yogis, those with great faith who always abide in Me, think of Me within their hearts, and render transcendental loving service to Me—they are the most intimately united with Me in yoga and are the highest of all. That is My opinion."

Here, at the end of the Sixth Chapter, Krishna informs us that the culmination of all kinds of yoga practice lies in *bhakti-yoga*, or transcendental loving service to Him. All other yogas are but means to come to the point of *bhakti* in *bhakti-yoga*. *Karma-yoga*, to work without fruitive results, is the beginning of this path. When *karma-yoga* increases in knowledge and renunciation, the stage is called *jnana-yoga*. When *jnana-yoga* increases in meditation on the Supersoul by different physical processes, and the mind is fixed on Him, it is called *astanga-yoga*. And when one surpasses *astanga-yoga* and comes to the point of the Supreme Person, Krishna, it is called *bhakti-yoga*, the highest stage of yoga and the ultimate goal.

7

Knowledge of the Absolute

IN THE FIRST SIX CHAPTERS of the *Bhagavad-gita*, Krishna has described the living entity as a non-material spirit soul capable of elevating itself to self-realization by different types of yoga. At the end of Chapter Six, Krishna clearly states that the steady concentration of the mind upon Him (bhakti yoga or Krishna consciousness) is the highest form of all yoga. In the next six chapters, Krishna will reveal scientific knowledge of Himself and the eternal relationship of the living entities with Him— revelations understood by the practice of *bhakti-yoga*.

The Supreme Lord
"Now hear, O Arjuna, how by practicing yoga in full consciousness of Me, with mind attached to Me, you can know Me in full, free from doubt.

"Out of many thousands of people, one may endeavor for perfection, and of those who have achieved perfection, hardly one knows Me in truth." Only pure devotees can know something of the inconceivable transcendental qualities of Krishna, of His omnipotence and opulence,

By watering the root of a tree, we water the whole tree—the twigs, branches, leaves, fruits, and flowers. Similarly, by loving Krishna we distribute our love to all living beings.

and of His wealth, fame, strength, beauty, knowledge, and renunciation, because Krishna reveals Himself to the devotees, being pleased with them for their transcendental loving service to Him.

Krishna describes His various energies. "Earth, water, fire, air, ether, mind, intelligence, and false ego—all together these eight constitute My separated material energies. Besides these, O mighty-armed Arjuna, there is another, superior energy of Mine, which comprises the living entities who are exploiting the resources of this material, inferior nature." As living entities we are His superior energy because the quality of our existence, as full with knowledge and eternal happiness, is the same as the Supreme Lord's. However, we are never equal to the Lord in quantity of power.

While exploiting the gross and subtle inferior energies, one forgets one's spiritual mind and intelligence and identifies oneself as the material body. This forgetfulness is due to the influence of matter upon us. But when we become free from the influence of the material energy, we are liberated from all material ideas, including the conception of becoming one in all respects with God.

"All created beings have their source in these two natures. Of all that is material and all that is spiritual in this world, know for certain that I am both the origin and dissolution." Everything that exists is a product of matter and spirit. This material body develops because spirit is present within

The Lord says that water,
earth, air—the basic
ingredients of this
planet—are His energy.

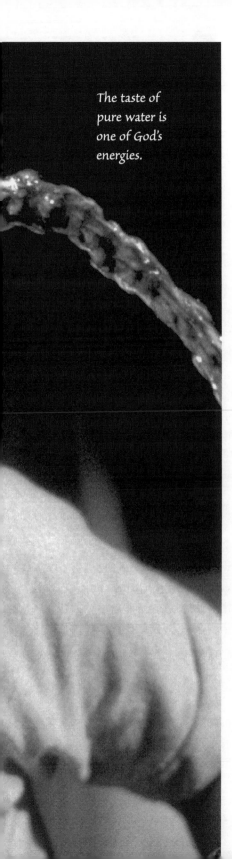

The taste of pure water is one of God's energies.

matter; a child grows gradually to become a teenager and then an adult because that superior energy, the soul, is present. Similarly, the entire universe develops because of the presence of Krishna as the Supersoul.

"O conqueror of wealth, there is no truth superior to Me. Everything rests upon Me, as pearls are strung on a thread. O Arjuna, I am the taste of water, the light of the sun and the moon, the syllable *om* in the Vedic mantras; I am the sound in ether and ability in people." Although the Lord is in His eternal abode, we can perceive Him by His diverse energies.

"I am the original fragrance of the earth, and I am the heat in fire. I am the life of all that lives, and I am the original seed of all existences, the intelligence of the intelligent, and the prowess of all powerful people.

"I am the strength of the strong, devoid of passion and desire. I am sex life which is not contrary to religious principles, O Arjuna."

The strong person should apply his strength to protect the weak, not for personal aggression. Sex life, according to religious principles, should be for the propagation of children, and the parents' responsibility is then to help their children become godly.

"Know that all states of being—be they goodness, passion or ignorance—are manifested by My energy. I am not under the modes of material nature, for they, on the contrary, are within Me." All material activities in the world are being conducted under the three modes of material nature—goodness, passion, and ignorance—which are emanations from the Supreme Lord. However, He is neither subjected to nor affected by these modes.

"This divine energy of Mine, consisting of the three modes of material nature, is difficult to overcome. But those who have surrendered unto Me can easily cross beyond it."

Krishna then describes four kinds of misdirected people who refuse to surrender to the Supreme: (1) those who are grossly foolish, (2) those who are socially and politically developed, but have no religious principles, (3) great philosophers, poets, literati, scientists, and others who deride God, considering Him merely another human being, and (4) those who are openly atheistic. Some atheists argue that the Supreme Lord can never descend into this material world, but they are unable to give any tangible reasons as to why not. Others make Him subordinate to His impersonal feature, although Krishna declares the opposite in the *Gita*. Envious of the Supreme Person, they cannot surrender to Him. Thus, these four types of impious people never surrender to the Supreme Lord, in spite of all scriptural and authoritative advice.

The humble ass works hard and is satisfied merely by filling his stomach.
Thus he is like the foolish worker who
does not know for whom he should
work or why. Sometimes this worker
may bray of poetry and philosophy,
but such sounds only disturb others.

As a policeman is empowered by the government he serves, demigods are empowered by the Supreme Lord.

"O Arjuna, four types of pious people begin to render devotional service unto Me—the distressed, the desirers of wealth, the sometimes inquisitive, and those who are searching for knowledge of the Absolute." Those who are always busy with fruitive activities come to the Lord in material distress and then associate with pure devotees and become, in their distress, devotees of the Lord. Those who are simply frustrated also come sometimes to associate with pure devotees and become inquisitive to know about God. Similarly, when dry philosophers are frustrated in every field of knowledge, they sometimes want to learn of God, and they come to the Supreme Lord to render devotional service. "Of these, those who are in full knowledge and who are always engaged in pure devotional service are the best. For I am very dear to them, and they are dear to Me.

"After many births and deaths, one who is actually in knowledge surrenders unto Me, knowing Me to be the cause of all causes and all that is. Such a great soul is very rare.

"Those whose intelligence has been stolen by material desires surrender unto demigods and follow the particular rules and regulations of worship according to their own natures. I am in everyone's heart as the Supersoul. As soon as one desires to worship some demigod, I make his faith steady so that he can devote himself to that particular deity. Endowed with such a faith, he endeavors to worship a particular demigod and obtains his desires. But in actuality these benefits are bestowed by Me alone." The demigods are powerful universal administrators who can bestow material benedictions upon those who worship them. Thus less intelligent people who have lost their spiritual sense take shelter of demigods for immediate fulfillment of material desires. Devotees, however, depend on the Supreme Lord for the satisfaction of their material needs, and are satisfied with whatever the Lord gives.

One may ask why all-powerful God gives facilities to the living entities for enjoying this world and lets them fall into the trap of the material energy. The answer is that if the Supreme Lord as Supersoul does not give such facilities, then there is no meaning to independence. Therefore He gives everyone full independence—whatever one likes—but His ultimate instruction in the *Bhagavad-gita* is: one should give up all other engagements and fully surrender unto Him. That will lead to happiness.

"People of small intelligence worship the demigods, and their fruits are limited and temporary. Those who worship the demigods go to the planets of the demigods, but My devotees ultimately reach My supreme planet.

"Unintelligent people, who do not know Me perfectly, think that I, the Supreme Lord, Krishna, was impersonal before and have now assumed this personality. Due to their small knowledge, they do not know My higher nature, which is imperishable and supreme." As demigod worshipers are less intelligent, so, too, are impersonal-ists—those who think that the Supreme Absolute Truth ultimately has no form. The impersonal feature is one of the Lord's aspects, as sunshine is an energy of the sun. Supreme realization may begin from this impersonal fea-ture and then rise to the localized Supersoul—but the ultimate word in the Absolute Truth is the Supreme Person, Lord Krishna.

"O Arjuna, as the Supreme Lord, I know everything that has happened in the past, all that is happening in the present, and all things that are yet to come. I also know all living entities; but Me no one knows.

"Those who have acted piously in previous lives and in this life and whose sinful actions are completely eradi-cated are freed from dualities and engage in My service with determination." For those who are sinful, atheistic, foolish, and deceitful, it is very difficult to transcend the dualities of material nature and advance spiritually.

But, Krishna says, "Those in full consciousness of Me, who know Me, the Supreme Lord, to be the governing principle of the material manifestation, of the demigods, and of all methods of sacrifice, can understand and know Me, the Supreme Person, even at the time of death."

When the sky is reflected in water, the reflections represent both the stars and the moon. The stars may be compared to the living entities, and the moon to the Supreme Lord. The Lord is the greatest Being, and the living entities are eternally small, both in the spiritual world and in its reflection, the material world.

8

Attaining the Supreme

Arjuna

O my Lord, O Supreme Person, what is Brahman? What is the self? What are fruitive activities? What is this material manifestation? And what are the demigods? Please explain this to me.

"Who is the Lord of sacrifice, and how does He live in the body, O Krishna? And how can those engaged in devotional service know You at the time of death?"

The Supreme Lord

"The indestructible, transcendental living entity is called Brahman [the individual soul], and its eternal nature is called the self. Action pertaining to the development of the material bodies of the living entities is called karma, or fruitive activities." Krishna is answering Arjuna's questions one by one. He explains that, under the influence of material consciousness, the living entity (Brahman) has to take on various bodies in the material world. That is karma, or varied creation by the force of material consciousness.

At the time of death, the soul—represented by the bird— leaves the cage of the body. As explained in this chapter, where the soul journeys depends on its consciousness.

Our thoughts at death result from our thoughts during life. Our final thoughts carry us—each soul—to the body we shall have next.

"The physical nature, which is constantly changing, is called the material manifestation. The universal form of the Lord includes all the demigods, like those of the sun and moon, and I, the Supreme Lord, represented as the Supersoul in the heart of every embodied being, am called the Lord of sacrifice." The Supersoul, who is non-different from the Supreme Lord Himself, is situated in the heart of every living entity beside the individual soul, as the witness of the individual soul's activities.

After briefly answering six of Arjuna's questions, the Lord answers at length his seventh and final question.

"Whoever, at the end of life, quits the body remembering Me alone, at once attains My nature. Of this there is no doubt." The thoughts during our lives accumulate to influence our thoughts at the moment of death. In this way our present life creates our next life. Those who die with their consciousness fixed on Krishna are at once transferred to the transcendental nature of the Supreme Lord. This remembrance of Krishna is possible for those who have been Krishna conscious during their lifetimes. Therefore, if we want to achieve success at the end of our lives, the process of remembering God is essential, and to this end devotees chant the Lord's holy names, which reawakens their God consciousness.

"One should meditate upon the Supreme Person as the one who knows everything, as He who is the oldest, who is the controller, who is smaller than the smallest, who is the maintainer of everything, who is beyond all material conception, who is inconceivable, and who is always a person. He is luminous like the sun, and He is transcendental, beyond this material nature.

"One who, at the time of death, fixes the life air between the eyebrows and, by the strength of yoga, with an undeviating mind, engages in remembering the

As a mannequin imitates a higher reality—a person—so this material world imitates the spiritual one.

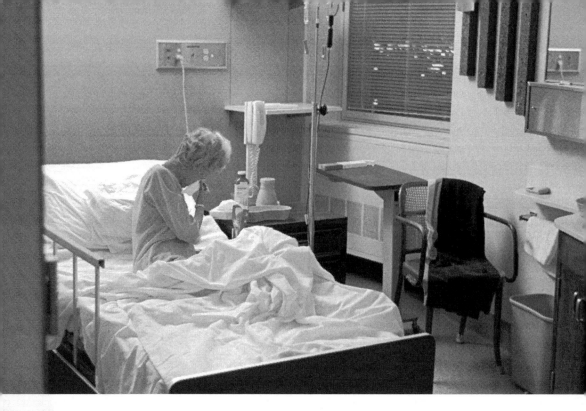

Supreme Lord in full devotion, will certainly attain to the Supreme Lord.

"After attaining Me, the great souls, who are yogis in devotion, never return to this temporary world, which is full of miseries, because they have attained the highest perfection. From the highest planet in the material world down to the lowest, all are places of misery wherein repeated birth and death take place. But one who attains My abode, O Arjuna, never takes birth again." Since this temporary material world is full of the miseries of birth, old age, disease, and death, naturally the person who attains God's kingdom does not wish to return. As God is transcendental and eternal, so is His kingdom. It is beyond all the periodic manifestations and annihilations of material nature.

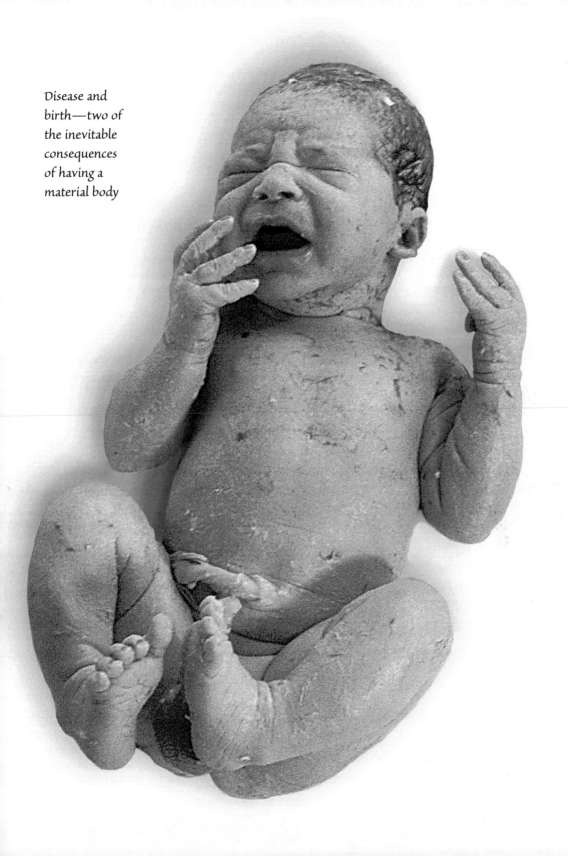

Disease and birth—two of the inevitable consequences of having a material body

"A person who accepts the path of devotional service is not bereft of the results derived from studying the *Vedas*, performing austere sacrifices, giving in charity, or pursuing philosophical and fruitive activities. Simply by performing devotional service, that person attains all these, and at the end reaches the supreme eternal abode." The beauty of Krishna consciousness is that by one stroke, by engaging in devotional service, we can surpass all the rituals of the different orders of life. We should try to understand this not by scholarship or mental speculation but by hearing about Krishna in association with devotees.

We can learn the *Bhagavad-gita* from a devotee, for no one else perfectly understands the purpose of the *Bhagavad-gita*. By such advancement in the association of the devotee, one is placed in devotional service and this service at once will dispel all one's misgivings about God and His activities, forms, pastimes, names, and other features. Then one becomes fixed in one's study, relishes that study, and always feels God conscious. In the advanced stage, one falls completely in love with God. This highest perfectional stage of life enables devotees to be transferred to the Lord's abode in the spiritual sky, where they become eternally happy.

As one can smell the fragrance of a rose by being near it, so the Supersoul—the Lord, seated in the heart next to the soul—knows the soul's innermost desires.

9

The Most Confidential Knowledge

KNOWLEDGE CONCERNING the eternal, constitutional activity of the soul, which is *bhakti*, or transcendental devotional service to God, is the most confidential knowledge because, although this knowledge is available to all, only a devotee will accept it. This is the subject of this chapter.

The Supreme Lord
"My dear Arjuna, because you are never envious of Me, I shall impart to you this most confidential knowledge and realization; knowing this you shall be relieved of the miseries of material existence." Simply to understand that a living entity is ultimately spiritual is insufficient. That is the beginning of spiritual realization, but we should recognize the difference between the activities of those who are bodily conscious and the activities of those who are spiritually conscious.

A woman with a paramour does her duties carefully, so that her husband won't suspect her attachment. Similarly, devotees always remember the supreme lover, Krishna, while seeing to their material duties.

As one controls the movements
of one's shadow, the Lord
controls the material energy.

"This knowledge is the king of education, the most secret of all secrets. It is the purest knowledge, and because it gives direct perception of the self by realization, it is the perfection of religion." There are huge colleges all over the world with many departments of knowledge. But there is, unfortunately, no college or educational institution that teaches the science of the spirit soul. Yet the soul is the most important part of the body; without the presence of the soul, the body has no value. Still people are placing all their energies on the bodily necessities of life, not caring for the vital soul.

The knowledge of which Krishna speaks leads to devotional service, a happy and sublime process, which, in His words, is "everlasting and joyfully performed." One can simply hear the chanting of the glories of the Lord or attend philosophical lectures on transcendental knowledge given by bona fide spiritual teachers. Simply by sitting, one can learn; then one can eat palatable food that has been offered to God. The prerequisite for this service isn't wealth, erudition, or an aristocratic birth, but only faith.

"Those who are not faithful in this devotional service cannot attain Me, O conqueror of enemies. Therefore they return to the path of birth and death in this material world." Faith is the conviction that simply by serving the Supreme Lord one can achieve all perfection.

"Understand that as the mighty wind, blowing everywhere, rests always in the sky, all created beings rest in Me. O Arjuna, at the end of the millennium all material manifestations enter into My nature, and at the

beginning of another millennium, by My potency, I create them again.

"The whole cosmic order is under Me. Under My will it is automatically manifested again and again, and under My will it is annihilated at the end.

"O Arjuna, all this work cannot bind Me. I am ever detached from all these material activities, seated as though neutral." In His spiritual world the Supreme Lord engages in His eternal, blissful, spiritual activities; He has nothing to do with material activities. Those are being carried on by His different potencies.

"This material nature, which is one of My energies, is working under My direction, O Arjuna, producing all moving and nonmoving beings. Under its rule this manifestation is created and annihilated again and again." Material nature, without the superintendence of the

A judge sends one person to the electric chair and awards another a sum of money, but the judge is impartial; the judgment depends on the case. Similarly, according to what we do, the impartial Lord awards us bitter or sweet fruits.

Supreme Lord, can do nothing. Yet the Supreme Lord is detached from all material activity.

"Fools deride Me when I descend in the human form. They do not know My transcendental nature as the Supreme Lord of all. Those who are thus bewildered are attracted by demonic and atheistic views. In that deluded condition, their hopes for liberation, their fruitive activities, and their culture of knowledge are all defeated.

"O Arjuna, those who are not deluded, the great souls, are under the protection of the divine nature. They are fully engaged in devotional service because they know Me as the Supreme Person, original and inexhaustible. Always chanting My glories, endeavoring with great determination, bowing down before Me, these great souls perpetually worship Me with devotion.

"I am the goal, the sustainer, the master, the witness, the abode, the refuge, and the most dear friend. I am the creation and the annihilation, the basis of everything, the resting place, and the eternal seed. O Arjuna, I give heat, and I withhold and send forth the rain. I am immortality, and I am also death personified. Both spirit and matter are in Me." By analyzing all of God's different energies, one can understand that for Him there is no distinction between matter and spirit. In the advanced stage of God consciousness, one therefore makes no such distinctions. A pure devotee sees only God in everything.

"Those who always worship Me with exclusive devotion, meditating on My transcendental form—to them I carry what they lack, and I preserve what they have." The Lord helps the devotees achieve God consciousness, and when they become fully God conscious, the Lord protects them from a miserable conditioned life.

"Those who are devotees of other gods and who worship them with faith actually worship only Me, O Arjuna, but they do so in a wrong way. I am the only enjoyer and master of all sacrifices. Therefore, those who do not recognize My true transcendental nature fall down. Those who worship the demigods will take birth among the demigods; those who worship the ancestors will go to the ancestors; those who worship ghosts and spirits will take birth among such beings; and those who worship Me will live with Me.

"If one offers Me with love and devotion a leaf, a flower, a fruit, or water, I will accept it." The process of Krishna consciousness is so easy that we can offer even a leaf or a little water or fruit to the Supreme Lord in genuine love, and the Lord will be pleased to accept it. No one, therefore, can be barred from Krishna consciousness, because it is so simple and universal. One who loves Krishna will give Him whatever pleases Him, and so a devotee avoids offering undesirable or unwanted things. Thus the devotee does not offer meat, fish, and eggs to Krishna. If He desired such things as offerings, He would have said so here. Vegetables, grains, fruits, milk, and water are the proper foods for human beings, and Lord Krishna Himself prescribes them.

Impersonalist philosophers, who believe that the Absolute Truth is without senses, cannot understand how the Lord eats. In actuality, Krishna, the Supreme Lord, has senses, and His senses are interchangeable; in other

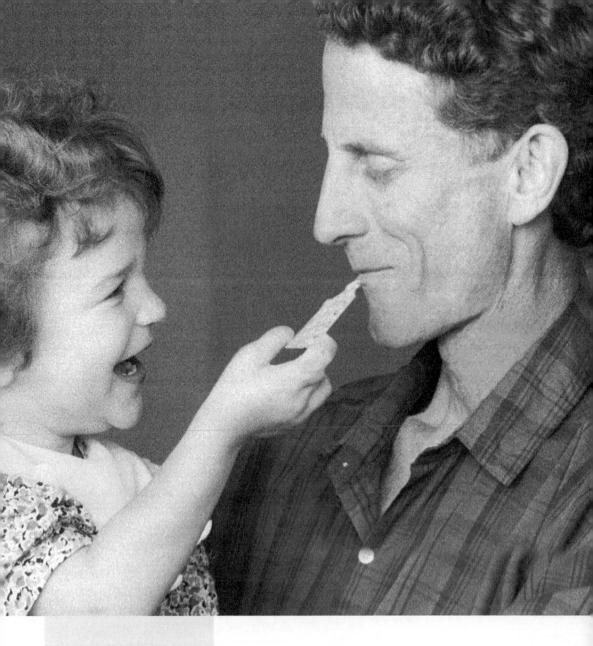

When a child lovingly offers her father a cracker, her father, who has no need for the cracker, is happy to accept it. In the same way, God is pleased when we first offer Him the food He has kindly provided.

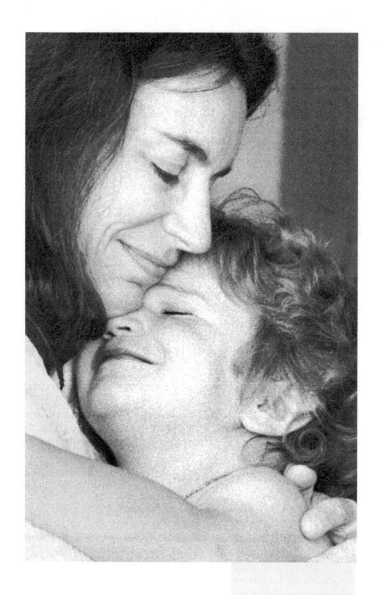

As soon as a child comes to the arms of her mother, the child's tears stop; she is happy. Similarly, when we love God we will feel completely happy.

words, one sense can perform the function of any other. This is what it means to say that Krishna is absolute. Lacking senses, He could hardly be considered full in all opulences. Krishna's hearing His devotee's words of love in the offering of food is wholly identical with His eating and tasting. Krishna wants only loving service and nothing more. He needs nothing from anyone, because He is self-sufficient, and yet He accepts the offering of His devotee in an exchange of love and affection. This love and devotion (*bhakti*) is the only means by which to approach Him.

"Whatever you do, whatever you eat, whatever you offer or give away, and whatever austerities you perform— do that, O Arjuna, as an offering to Me. In this way you will be freed from bondage to work and its auspicious and inauspicious results. With your mind fixed on Me in this principle of renunciation, you will be liberated and come to Me.

"Even those who commit the most abominable action, if they are engaged in devotional service they are considered saintly because they are properly situated in their determination." Material contamination is so strong that even a yogi fully absorbed in the service of the Lord sometimes becomes ensnared; but Krishna consciousness is so strong that such an occasional lapse into bodily identification is at once rectified. No one should deride a devotee for some accidental lapse. On the other hand, we should not think that a devotee can act in all kinds of abominable ways; this statement by Krishna only refers to an accident due to the strong power of material connections.

"They quickly become righteous and attain lasting peace. O Arjuna, declare it boldly that My devotees never perish.

"O Arjuna, those who take shelter in Me, though they be of lower birth, can attain the supreme destination. Therefore, having come to this temporary world, engage in loving service unto Me." Here the Supreme Lord clearly makes no distinction between lower and higher classes of people engaged in His devotional service. Such divisions exist in the material conception of life, but not for a person engaged in the Lord's transcendental service. Through this pure loving service, everyone can become attached to God, and anyone may enter His kingdom. Devotional service to the Supreme Lord is the process by which all people can solve all problems.

"Engage your mind always in thinking of Me, become My devotee, offer obeisances to Me, and worship Me. Being completely absorbed in Me, surely you will come to Me."

When a mother sees her child's shoes, she remembers the child she loves. In the same way, when the Lord's pure devotees see anything in this world, they are reminded of their beloved Lord.

10

The Opulence of the Absolute

The Supreme Lord

LISTEN AGAIN, O MIGHTY-ARMED ARJUNA. Because you are My dear friend, for your benefit I shall speak to you further." In this chapter, Krishna will explain His specific opulences, manifested through His all-pervasive energies.

"I am the source of all spiritual and material worlds. Everything emanates from Me. The wise who perfectly know this engage in My devotional service and worship Me with all their hearts.

Arjuna

"You are the Supreme Person, the ultimate abode, the purest, the Absolute Truth. You are the eternal, transcendental, original person, the unborn, the greatest. All the great sages such as Narada, Asita, Devala, and Vyasa confirm this truth about You, and now You Yourself are declaring it to me.

"O Krishna, I totally accept as truth all that You have told me. Neither the demigods nor the demons,

God's opulences are the smallest wonders and the greatest majesties of our world.

O Lord, can understand Your personality. Indeed, You alone know Yourself by Your own internal potency, O Supreme Person.

"Please tell me in detail of Your divine opulences by which You pervade all these worlds. O Krishna, how shall I constantly think of You, and how shall I know You? In what various forms shall I remember You, O Supreme Person? Again please describe in detail the mystic power of Your opulences." Arjuna has no doubt about Krishna's supremacy, but he wants to know how the common person can understand the all-pervading Lord. Common people who have no love for God cannot always think of Him; therefore they have to think materially. Because materialists cannot understand Krishna spiritually, Krishna advises them to concentrate their minds on physical things and try to see how He manifests Himself through them.

The Supreme Lord
"Yes, I will tell you of My splendorous manifestations, but only of those which are prominent, O Arjuna, for My opulence is limitless.

"Of lights I am the radiant sun. Of the senses I am the mind, and in living beings I am consciousness. Of bodies of water I am the ocean; of vibrations I am the transcendental *om*." Of all the transcendental sound vibrations, the sacred syllable *om* (*omkara*) represents Krishna. "Of sacrifices I am the chanting of the holy names [*japa*]." Of all sacrifices, the chanting of Krishna's holy names is the purest representation of God. "Of immovable things I am

the Himalayas."
Whatever is sublime
in the world is a repre-
sentation of Krishna.
Therefore the
Himalayas, the greatest
mountains in the world,
also represent Him.

"Of all trees I am the
banyan tree, and of the
sages among the
demigods I am Narada.
Among subduers I am
inexhaustible time,
among beasts I am the
lion, and among birds I
am Garuda." The banyan
tree is one of the highest
and most beautiful trees.
Narada is considered the
greatest devotee in the
universe, thus Krishna
chooses him as the
representation of a
pure devotee. Among
many subduing princi-
ples, time wears down all
things in the material
universe and so
represents Krishna. Of

Of lights He is the sun,
and of bodies of water He
is the ocean.

animals, the lion is the most powerful and ferocious, and of the million varieties of birds, Garuda, the bearer of Lord Vishnu, is the greatest.

"Of purifiers I am the wind, of the wielders of weapons I am Rama, of fishes I am the shark, and of flowing rivers I am the Ganges." Of all the aquatics the shark is one of the biggest and is certainly the most dangerous to man. Thus the shark represents Krishna.

"Of all creations I am the beginning and the end and also the middle, O Arjuna. Of all sciences I am the spiritual science of the self, and among logicians I am the conclusive truth. I am all-devouring death, and I am the generating principle of all that is yet to be. Among women I

If death is like a cat, then a devotee is like a kitten, carried to safety.

Of seasons, Krishna is flower-bearing spring.

am fame, fortune, fine speech, memory, intelligence, steadfastness, and patience." When a person is fully qualified, yet humble and gentle, and when she is able to keep her balance both in sorrow and in the ecstasy of joy, she has the opulence called patience.

"Of seasons I am flower-bearing spring. I am also the gambling of cheats." There are many kinds of cheaters, but of all cheating processes, gambling stands supreme and therefore represents Krishna. As the Supreme, Krishna can be more deceitful than any mere mortal. If Krishna chooses to deceive a person, no one can surpass Him in His deceit. His greatness is not simply one-sided— it is all-sided.

"Of the splendid I am the splendor. I am victory, I am adventure, and I am the strength of the strong." He is the most splendorous of all. Among the enterprising and industrious, He is the most enterprising, the most industrious. No one can surpass Him.

"Among all means of suppressing lawlessness I am punishment, and of those who seek victory I am morality." When miscreants are punished, the agency of chastisement represents Krishna. In any attempt at being victorious in some field of activity, the greatest element is morality.

"Of secret things I am silence, and of the wise I am wisdom." Among the confidential activities of hearing, thinking, and meditating, silence is most important

God's greatness is not simply one-sided—it is all-sided. If He chooses to deceive a person, no one can surpass Him in His deceit. And of all forms of cheating, gambling stands supreme and therefore represents Krishna.

because by silence one can make progress quickly. The wise person is one who can discriminate between matter and spirit, between God's inferior and superior natures. Such knowledge is Krishna Himself. "Furthermore, O Arjuna, I am the generating seed of all existences. O mighty conqueror of enemies, there is no end to My divine manifestations. What I have spoken to you is but a mere indication of My infinite opulences.

"Know that all opulent, beautiful, and glorious creations spring from but a spark of My splendor. But what need is there, Arjuna, for all this detailed knowledge? With a single fragment of Myself I pervade and support this entire universe." The Supersoul enters into all things and represents the Supreme Lord throughout the material universes. The Lord here tells Arjuna that there is no point in understanding how anything exists in its separate opulence and grandeur; all things are existing, from the most gigantic entity down to the smallest ant, due to His entering them as Supersoul, and all are sustained by Him. Therefore Lord Krishna is worshipable.

11

The Universal Form

Arjuna

B Y HEARING FROM YOU my illusion has now been dispelled and I have realized Your inexhaustible glories." Now Arjuna no longer sees Krishna as merely a human being, or only as his friend, but rather as the source of everything. Arjuna is enlightened. He is glad to have such a great friend as Krishna, but he thinks that, while he accepts Krishna as the source of everything, others may not. So to establish Krishna's divinity for all, in this chapter he requests that Krishna show His universal form.

"O greatest of all personalities, though I see You here before me in Your actual position, as You have described Yourself, I wish to see how You have entered into this cosmic manifestation. I want to see that form of Yours. If You think that I am able to behold Your cosmic form, O my Lord, O Master of all mystic power, then kindly show me that unlimited universal Self." Arjuna, as a devotee, does not depend on his speculative strength; rather, he admits his limitations as a living entity and acknowledges

If you have a loving father who is a policeman, one day you may see him in action, firing his revolver. At that time, awe and fear overcome your love. In the same way, when Arjuna saw Krishna's cosmic form, he was frightened. Thus he requested Krishna to appear again in a form he could love.

Krishna's inestimable position. Arjuna knows that the infinitesimal living entity cannot understand the unlimited infinite. If the infinite reveals Himself, only then is it possible to understand the nature of the infinite, by the grace of the infinite.

If hundreds of
thousands of
suns were to
rise at once into
the sky, their
radiance might
resemble the
effulgence of
the Supreme
Person in His
universal form.

The Supreme Person
"My dear Arjuna, see now My opulences, hundreds of
thousands of varied divine and multicolored forms.
Behold the many wonderful things which no one has ever
seen or heard of before.

"O Arjuna, this universal form can show you whatever you now desire to see and whatever you may want to see in the future. Everything—moving and nonmoving—is here completely, in one place.

"But you cannot see Me with your present eyes. Therefore I give you divine eyes. Behold My mystic opulence!"

Arjuna saw in that universal form unlimited mouths, unlimited eyes, unlimited wonderful visions. The form was decorated with many celestial ornaments and bore many divine upraised weapons. He wore celestial garlands and garments, and many divine scents were smeared over His body. All was wondrous, brilliant, unlimited, all-expanding.

At that time Arjuna could see in the universal form of the Lord the unlimited expansions of the universe

The demigods offer prayers to the universal form of the Lord.

situated in one place although divided into many, many thousands.

Then, bewildered and astonished, his hair standing on end, Arjuna bowed his head to offer obeisances and with folded hands began to pray to the Supreme Lord.

Arjuna
"My dear Lord Krishna, I see assembled in Your body all the demigods and various other living entities. O universal form, I see in Your body many, many arms, bellies, mouths, and eyes, expanded everywhere, without limit. Your form is difficult to see because of its glaring effulgence, spreading on all sides, like blazing fire or the immeasurable radiance of the sun. I see this glowing form everywhere, adorned with various crowns, clubs, and discs.

"You are the supreme primal objective. You are the ultimate resting place of all this universe. You are inexhaustible, and You are the oldest. You are the maintainer

of the eternal religion, the Supreme Person. This is my opinion.

"You are without origin, middle, or end. Your glory is unlimited. You have numberless arms, and the sun and moon are Your eyes. I see You with blazing fire coming forth from Your mouth, burning this entire universe by Your own radiance.

"All the hosts of demigods are surrendering before You and entering into You. Some of them, very much afraid, are offering prayers with

Arjuna sees an unlimited number of faces in the universal form.

folded hands. Hosts of great sages and perfected beings, crying 'All peace!' are praying to You by singing the Vedic hymns.

"O all-pervading Vishnu, as I gaze upon You with Your radiant colors touching the sky, Your gaping mouths, and Your great glowing eyes, my mind is perturbed by fear. Seeing Your blazing deathlike faces and awful teeth I can no longer maintain my steadiness or equilibrium of mind. In all directions I am bewildered.

"All the sons of Dhritarastra, along with their allied kings—and our chief soldiers also—are rushing into Your fearful mouths. And some I see trapped with heads smashed between Your teeth. As the many waves of the rivers flow into the ocean, so do all these great warriors enter blazing into Your mouths. I see all people rushing full speed into Your mouths, as moths dash to destruction in a blazing fire.

"O Lord of lords, so fierce of form, please tell me who You are. I offer my obeisances unto You; please be gracious to me. I want to know about You, for I do not know Your mission."

The Supreme Lord
"Time I am, the great destroyer of the worlds, and I have come here to destroy all people. With the exception of you [Arjuna and his four brothers], all the soldiers here on both sides will be slain. Therefore get up. Prepare to fight and win glory. Conquer your enemies and enjoy a flourishing kingdom. They are already put to death by My arrangement, and you, O Arjuna, can be but an

instrument in the fight. Kill them and do not be disturbed." The whole world moves according to the plan of the Supreme Lord. Those with insufficient knowledge think that nature is moving without a plan and that all manifestations are but accidental formations. But in fact this cosmic manifestation is a chance for the conditioned souls to go back to God's kingdom, to go back home. Those who follow His plan are victorious in the struggle for existence.

Arjuna
"The world becomes joyful upon hearing Your name, and thus everyone becomes attached to You. Although the perfected beings offer You their respectful homage, the demons are afraid, and they flee here and there. All this is rightly done. You are the original creator. O limitless one, God of gods, refuge of the universe! You are the invincible

source, the cause of all causes, transcendental to this material manifestation. Thinking of You as my friend, I have rashly addressed You, 'O Krishna,' 'O my friend,' not knowing Your glories. Please forgive whatever I may have done in madness or in love. I have dishonored You many times, jesting as we relaxed, lay on the same bed, or sat or ate together, sometimes alone and sometimes in front of

Arjuna

many friends. O infallible one, please excuse me for all those offenses.

"As a father tolerates the impudence of his son, or a friend tolerates the impertinence of a friend, or a wife tolerates the familiarity of her partner, please tolerate the wrongs I may have done to You.

"After seeing this universal form, which I have never seen before, I am gladdened, but at the same time my mind is disturbed with fear. Therefore please bestow Your grace upon me and reveal again Your form as the Supreme Person, O Lord of lords, O abode of the universe."

The Supreme Person
"My dear Arjuna, happily have I shown you this supreme universal form within the material world. No one before you has ever seen this primal form, unlimited and full of glaring effulgence. Not by studying the Vedas, nor by performing sacrifices, nor by charity, nor by pious activities, nor by severe penances can I be seen in this form.

"You have been perturbed and bewildered by seeing this horrible feature of Mine. Now let it be finished. My devotee, be free again from all disturbances. With a peaceful mind you can now see the form you desire." The Supreme Person, Krishna, displays His four-armed form and at last shows His two-armed form, thus encouraging Arjuna.

Arjuna
"O Krishna, seeing this humanlike form, so very beautiful, I am now composed in mind, and I am restored to my original nature."

The Supreme Person

"My dear Arjuna, this form of Mine you are now seeing is very difficult to behold. Even the demigods are ever seeking the opportunity to see this form, which is so dear.

"The form you are seeing with your transcendental eyes cannot be understood simply by studying the Vedas, nor by undergoing serious penances, nor by charity, nor by worship. It is not by these means that one can see Me as I am.

"My dear Arjuna, only by undivided devotional service can I be understood as I am, standing before you, and can thus be seen directly. Only in this way can you enter into the mysteries of My understanding." Krishna changes from the universal form to the four-handed form of Narayana and then to His own natural two-handed form. The original two-handed Krishna is the origin of all emanations. Therefore one should conclusively worship the Supreme Lord, Krishna, who has an eternal form of bliss and knowledge. He is the source of all forms of Vishnu, He is the source of all incarnations, and He is the original Supreme Person.

"My dear Arjuna, one who engages in My pure devotional service, free from the contaminations of fruitive activities and mental speculation, one who works for Me, who makes Me the supreme goal of life, and who is friendly to every living being—that person certainly comes to Me."

There are many examples in history of the Lord's devotees who risked their lives to spread God consciousness. A familiar example is Jesus Christ. He was crucified by nondevotees, but he sacrificed his life to spread Krishna consciousness. Similarly, in India there are also many examples, such as Thakura Haridasa and Prahlada Maharaja. Why take such risk? Because they were convinced of the value of God conscious-

Lord Krishna

ness, and wanted to give it to others. Imagine how merciful God is to those engaged in His service, to those who risk everything for Him. Certainly such persons must go to Him after leaving their bodies.

In summary, Krishna has exhibited His universal form (which is a temporary manifestation), His form of time which devours everything, and even His four-handed form of Vishnu. Thus Krishna is the origin of all these manifestations and forms. Those who are attached to the original form of the Lord in love and devotion can see Him always within their hearts.

12

Devotional Service

Arjuna

WHICH ARE CONSIDERED to be more perfect, those who are always properly engaged in Your devotional service or those who worship the impersonal Brahman, the unmanifested?" Those who worship the Supreme Lord directly by engagement in devotional service are called personalists, while those who meditate on the impersonal energy of the Lord, which is beyond the reach of the senses, are called impersonalists.

The Supreme Person

"Those who fix their minds on My personal form and are always engaged in worshiping Me with great and transcendental faith are considered by Me to be most perfect." In answer to Arjuna's question, Krishna says that those who concentrate upon His personal form and worship Him with faith and devotion are most perfect in yoga.

The three stages of God realization are compared to seeing a hillside from different distances. Realization of the all-pervasive impersonal energy of the Lord (Brahman) is like seeing a misty hill from a great distance. Realization of the localized Supersoul (Paramatma) within the heart of every living entity is like recognizing specific forms on the hillside. And realization of the Supreme Person is like personally meeting the individual who lives on the hill. This is called Bhagavan realization and is the highest.

"For those whose minds are attached to the unmanifested, impersonal feature of the Supreme, advancement is very troublesome. To make progress in that discipline is always difficult for those who are embodied." A devotee has no difficulty in approaching the Supreme immediately and directly, whereas the impersonal path to spiritual realization is difficult, with the inherent risk of not realizing the Absolute Truth at the end. Krishna advises against this process. Impersonal realization contradicts the nature of the spiritual, blissful living soul. For every individual

Krishna compares material existence to an ocean in which the living entities suffer.

living entity the process of Krishna consciousness, which entails full engagement in devotional service, is the best and surest path.

"But those who worship Me, giving up all their activities unto Me and being devoted to Me without deviation, engaged in devotional service and always meditating upon Me, having fixed their minds upon Me, O Arjuna—for them I am the swift deliverer from the ocean of birth and death." It does not matter in what kind of work we engage, but we should do that work only as an offering to Krishna. The process is very simple: we can devote ourselves to Krishna in our occupations and at the same time

A letter in a mailbox authorized by the post office will go to its destination, while a letter in some homemade box will not go anywhere. Similarly, worship of a form of the Lord authorized in scripture is received by the Lord; worship of an imaginary, inauthentic form goes nowhere.

engage in chanting Hare Krishna, Hare Krishna, Krishna Krishna, Hare Hare / Hare Rama, Hare Rama, Rama Rama, Hare Hare. The Supreme Lord promises that without delay He will deliver a pure devotee thus engaged from the cycle of birth, death, and rebirth.

"Just fix your mind upon Me, the Supreme Person, and engage all your intelligence in Me. Thus you will live in Me always, without a doubt.

"My dear Arjuna, if you cannot fix your mind upon Me without deviation, then follow the regulative principles of *bhakti-yoga*. In this way develop a desire to attain Me." Love of God exists in a dormant state in everyone's heart. This love manifests in different ways, but it is contaminated by material association. However, through regulative principles, we can purify our hearts of this material association and revive our dormant love for Krishna. That is the process of *bhakti-yoga*.

To practice the regulative principles of *bhakti-yoga* we should, under the guidance of an expert spiritual master, follow certain principles: we should rise early in the morning, take a bath, enter the temple (which can be in the home), offer prayers and chant the Lord's holy names, take food that has been offered to the Lord, and hear or read the *Bhagavad-gita As It Is*. These practices help us rise to the level of love of God and then progress into the spiritual kingdom of God.

"If you cannot practice the regulations of *bhakti-yoga*, then just try to work for Me, because by working for Me you will come to the perfect stage." If we cannot directly practice the regulative principles of *bhakti-yoga*, we can try to help those who are propagating *bhakti-yoga*.

"If, however, you are unable to work in this consciousness of Me, then try to act giving up all results of your work and try to be self-situated." It may be that a person is unable even to sympathize with the activities of Krishna consciousness because of social, family, or religious considerations. Krishna advises that such persons give in charity or serve some good cause. Thus they may be gradually elevated to the state of knowledge. By giving in charity to a hospital or to some other social institution, or by performing community or national service, we may purify our minds of material desires and illusions and, in that purified state, gradually come to understand God. Of course, awareness of God is not dependent on any other experience, because this awareness in and of itself can purify the mind, but if impediments still remain in accepting God consciousness, then we may choose to give up the results of our actions as an indirect offering to God.

"One who is not envious but is a kind friend to all living entities, who does not think of oneself as a proprietor and who is free from false ego, who is equal in both happiness and distress, who is tolerant, always satisfied,

Some philosophers propose that the material creation is false, but this is not supported by the Bhagavad-gita. Just as a meal is real, although temporary, so is the material creation.

self-controlled, and engaged in devotional service with determination, with mind and intelligence fixed on Me—such a devotee of Mine is very dear to Me.

"One who is equal to friends and enemies, who is equipoised in honor and dishonor, heat and cold, happiness and distress, fame and infamy, who is always free from contaminating association, always silent and satisfied with anything, who doesn't care for any residence, who is fixed in knowledge, and who is engaged in devotional service—such a person is very dear to Me." Such a standard of devotional service is undoubtedly very rare, but a devotee becomes situated in that stage by following the regulative principles of devotional service.

"Those who follow this imperishable path of devotional service and who completely engage themselves with faith, making Me the supreme goal, are very, very dear to Me." The question of who is better—one who is engaged in the path of impersonal Brahman or one who is engaged in the personal service of the Supreme Lord—was raised by Arjuna, and the Lord replies so explicitly that there is no doubt that devotional service to the Lord is the best of all processes of spiritual realization. As long as we do not have the chance to associate with a pure devotee, the impersonal conception may be beneficial. But by hearing from or reading the words of a pure devotee, we develop directly a desire to engage in Krishna consciousness in pure devotional service, and this devotional service is the path for self-realization.

Trees are an emblem of tolerance, for they silently endure all inconveniences and yet continue to offer their soothing shelter to all.

13

Nature, the Enjoyer and Consciousness

STARTING WITH CHAPTER THIRTEEN, Krishna explains how the living entity comes into contact with material nature, how it is delivered, and how, although the living entity is completely different from the material body, they are related.

Arjuna
"O my dear Krishna, I wish to know about nature, the enjoyer, and the field and the knower of the field, and of knowledge and the object of knowledge."

The Supreme Person
"This body, O Arjuna, is called the field, and one who knows this body is called the knower of the field. You should understand that I am also the knower in all bodies, and to understand this body and its knower is called knowledge. That is My opinion." Here Lord Krishna presents three different topics of study: the Lord, the living entity, and matter. In every field of activity, in every body,

Krishna compares the body to a field and the soul to the field's owner. The products of the field depend upon the desires of the owner.

exist two souls: the individual soul and the Supersoul, the Supreme Lord. We may be the knower of our own body, but we are not in knowledge of other bodies. The Supreme Lord, who is present as the Supersoul in all bodies, knows everything about all bodies. He knows all the different bodies of all the various species of life.

The Lord then explains that twenty items constitute knowledge. "Humility; pridelessness; nonviolence; tolerance; simplicity; approaching a bona fide spiritual master; cleanliness; steadiness; self-control; renunciation of the objects of sense gratification; absence of false ego; the perception of the evil of birth, death, old age, and disease; detachment; freedom from entanglement with children, spouse, home, and the rest; even-mindedness amid pleasant and unpleasant events; constant and unalloyed devotion to Me; aspiring to live in a solitary place; detachment from the general mass of people; accepting the importance of self-realization; and philosophical search for the Absolute Truth—all these I declare to be knowledge, and besides this, whatever there may be is ignorance."

Of all these descriptions of the process of knowledge, the most important point is unalloyed devotional service to the Lord. If we do not approach the transcendental service of the Lord, then the other nineteen items mentioned here are of no particular value. In this regard, the principle of accepting a spiritual master is essential. Even if we take to devotional service, it is most important. Transcendental life begins when we accept a bona fide spiritual master. Then, beginning from humility, we gradually reawaken our spiritual knowledge, realize that we are subordinate to the Supreme Lord and that, due to rebelling against Him, we have become subordinate to material nature.

"I shall now explain the knowable, knowing which you will taste the eternal. The individual soul is beginningless and subordinate to Me, and lies beyond the cause and effect of this material world.

"The Supersoul pervades everything: everywhere are His hands and legs, His eyes, heads, and faces, and He has

What is commonly called "instinct" is the direction of the Supersoul—God in the heart of every living being.

ears everywhere. The Supersoul is the original source of all senses, yet He is without material senses. He is unattached, although He is the maintainer of all living beings. He transcends the modes of nature, and at the same time He is the master of all the modes of material nature."

The Supreme is different from the individual soul. The Supreme Lord can extend His hand without limit; the individual soul cannot. The Supreme Lord's senses are transcendental; they are not materially covered, as the individual soul's are. With our material senses we cannot see or understand Him, but when we purify our senses and minds by practicing Krishna consciousness, we can see Him constantly.

"The Supreme Truth exists outside and inside of all living beings, the moving and the nonmoving. Because He is subtle, He is beyond the power of the material senses to see or to know. Although far, far away, He is also near to all.

"Although the Supersoul appears to be divided among all beings, He is never divided. He is situated as one. He is the source of light in all luminous objects. He is beyond the darkness of matter and is unmanifested. He is knowledge, He is the object of

As the sun simultaneously appears in many water pots, yet remains one, the Supreme Lord resides within every body, beside the living being, yet He remains the one Supreme Person.

knowledge, and He is the goal of knowledge. He is situated in everyone's heart."

Thus Krishna has described the field of activity (the
body), the process of understanding, and both the soul
and the Supersoul. "Only My devotees can understand
this thoroughly and thus attain My nature."

The body is the field of activity and is composed of
material nature. The individual living entity (the soul) is

The conditioned soul is helplessly kicked from one body to another, just as a soccer ball is kicked on the playing field.

embodied and enjoys the activities of the body. The living entity is one knower, and the Supersoul is the other. Both the individual living entity and the Supersoul are different manifestations of the Supreme Lord. The living entity is His energy, and the Supersoul is His personal expansion.

"Nature is said to be the cause of all material causes and effects, whereas the living entity is the cause of the various sufferings and enjoyments in this world. The living

entities in material nature thus follow the ways of life, enjoying the three modes of material nature. This is due to their association with that material nature. Thus they meet with good and evil amongst various species."

According to our desires and activities, material nature places us in certain bodies, or residential quarters. Material happiness and distress are due to our bodies, and not to ourselves as a spirit soul. In our original state there is no doubt of eternal pleasure; that is our real state.

"Those who understand this philosophy concerning material nature, the living entity, and the interaction of the modes of nature are sure to attain liberation. Such persons will not take birth here again, regardless of their present position.

"O Arjuna, know that whatever you see in existence, both the moving and the nonmoving, is only a combination of the field of activities and the knower of the field.

"One who sees the Supersoul accompanying the individual soul in all bodies, and who understands that neither the soul nor the Supersoul within the destructible body is ever destroyed, actually sees." After the destruction of the body, both the soul and the Supersoul exist, and they continue eternally in various moving and nonmoving forms.

> With the body, we acquire senses which are drawn to certain sense objects. Thus a hog sees stool as a palatable meal.

"Those who see the Supersoul equally present everywhere, in every living being, do not degrade themselves by their minds. Thus they approach the transcendental destination." Our minds are generally addicted to the endless process of sense gratification; but when we turn our minds to the Supersoul, we become advanced in spiritual understanding.

"Those who see that all activities are performed by the body, which is created of material nature, and see that the self does nothing, actually see." We are forced to act—either for happiness or distress—by our bodily constitutions. The self, however, is outside all bodily activities.

"O Arjuna, as the sun alone illuminates all this universe, so does the living entity, one within the body, illuminate the entire body by consciousness.

"Those who see with eyes of knowledge the difference between the body and the knower of the body, and who can also understand the process of liberation from bondage in material nature, attain to the supreme goal." When we can see the constitution of the whole material manifestation as this combination of the soul and material elements, and when we can also see the situation of the Supreme Soul, we become eligible for transfer to the spiritual world. We are meant to contemplate and realize these things, and we can have a complete understanding of this chapter with the help of a self-realized spiritual master.

The soul and the Supersoul within the body resemble two birds sitting as friends in a tree. The conditioned soul tries to enjoy the fruits of the body, while the Supersoul simply watches, waiting for His friend to turn to Him.

The symptoms of
the mode of
passion are great
attachment and
unlimited desires
and longings.
Passion typically
governs the
relationship
between a man
and a woman.

14

The Three Modes of Material Nature

IN THE PREVIOUS CHAPTER, we understood that knowledge frees us from material entanglement and that association with the modes of nature entangles us in this material world. Now, in this chapter, the Supreme Lord explains what those modes of nature are, how they act, how they bind, and how they liberate. One who understands this chapter will attain perfection.

The Supreme Lord
"Again I shall declare to you this supreme wisdom, the best of all knowledge, knowing which all the sages have attained the supreme perfection. By becoming fixed in this knowledge, one can attain to the transcendental nature like My own. Thus established, one is not born at the time of creation or disturbed at the time of dissolution."

Such liberated souls reach the transcendental planets of the spiritual sky and there continue to engage in the Lord's transcendental loving service. There they have spiritual forms, engage in spiritual activities, and experience spiritual relationships.

"The total material substance is the source of birth, and it is that substance that I impregnate, making possible the births of all living beings, O Arjuna." The Supreme Lord Himself makes the combination of material nature and the living entity possible. Material nature is not the cause of the birth of the living entities. The Supreme Lord gives the seed, and the living entities only appear to be products of material nature. Thus, every living entity, according to its past activities, receives and inhabits a different body, created by material nature.

People used to believe that scorpions were born of rice. Now we know that scorpions grow from eggs laid in the rice. Similarly, material nature is not the cause of birth for the living entities. Living beings appear to be products of matter, but in truth the Supreme Lord is the seed-giving father.

"Understand that all species of life are made possible by birth in this material nature, and that I am the seed-giving father." The Supreme Lord is the original father of all living entities. Material nature, which provides the bodies of all living entities, is the mother. Thus the material world is impregnated by the Lord with living entities, who appear in various forms at the time of creation according to their past deeds.

"Material nature consists of three modes—goodness, passion, and

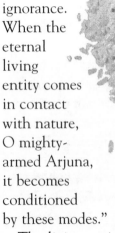

ignorance.
When the
eternal
living
entity comes
in contact
with nature,
O mighty-
armed Arjuna,
it becomes
conditioned
by these modes."

The living entity,
because it is transcendental,
has nothing to do with this material
world. Still, because it has become conditioned
by the material world, it must act under the spell of the
three modes of material nature. This is the cause of the
varieties of happiness and distress.

"O sinless one, the mode of goodness, being purer than
the others, is illuminating, and it frees one from all sinful
reactions. Those situated in that mode become conditioned by a sense of happiness and knowledge.

"The mode of passion is born of unlimited desires and
longings, and because of this the embodied living entity is
bound to material fruitive actions.

"O Arjuna, know that the mode of darkness, born of
ignorance, is the delusion of all embodied living entities.
The results of this mode are madness, indolence, and
sleep, which bind the conditioned soul.

"O Arjuna, the mode of goodness conditions one to happiness; passion conditions one to fruitive action; and ignorance, covering one's knowledge, binds one to madness.

"Sometimes the mode of goodness becomes prominent, defeating the modes of passion and ignorance. Sometimes the mode of passion defeats goodness and ignorance, and at other times ignorance defeats goodness and passion. In this way there is always competition for supremacy."

The characteristics of a specific mode of nature are in our activities, in eating, working, recreation, and so forth. By the quality of our activities, we can understand in what mode of nature we are situated.

"The manifestation of the mode of goodness can be experienced when one is illuminated by knowledge. O Arjuna, when there is an increase in the mode of passion, the symptoms of great attachment, fruitive activity, intense endeavor, uncontrollable desire, and hankering develop. When there is an increase in the mode of ignorance, darkness, inertia, madness, and illusion manifest.

"When one dies in the mode of goodness, one attains to the pure higher planets of the great sages. When one dies in the mode of passion, one takes birth among those engaged in fruitive activities; and when one dies in the mode of ignorance, one takes birth in the animal kingdom.

"When one properly sees that in all activities no performer is at work other than these modes of nature and one knows the Supreme Lord, who is transcendental to all these modes, one attains My spiritual nature."

A vulture flies high in the sky, but merely in search of a carcass. Similarly, we attain the exalted human birth, but, influenced by the modes of nature, we seek happiness in matter instead of spirit.

Arjuna
"O my dear Lord, by which symptoms is one known
who is transcendental to these three modes? What is
one's behavior? And how does one transcend the modes
of nature?"

The Supreme Person
"O son of Pandu, one who does not hate illumination,
attachment, and delusion when they are present or long
for them when they disappear; who is unwavering and
undisturbed through all these reactions of the material
qualities, remaining neutral and transcendental, knowing
that the modes alone are active; who is situated in the self
and regards as alike happiness and distress; who looks
upon a lump of earth, a stone, and a piece of gold with an
equal eye; who is equal toward the desirable and the undesirable; who is steady, situated equally well in praise and
blame, honor and dishonor; who treats alike both friend
and enemy; and who has renounced all material activities—
such a person has transcended the modes of nature."

As far as the symptoms of those who are transcendentally situated, the Lord states that such persons have no
envy and do not hanker for anything. We do not need
these material bodies, nor do we need to accept their dictates. The material modes of nature will act on the body,
but as spirit soul the self is aloof from such demands.

How do we become aloof? We desire neither to enjoy
the body, nor to be free of it. Thus transcendentally situated, the devotees become automatically free of the influence of material illusion. They see everything equally
because they know perfectly well that they have nothing

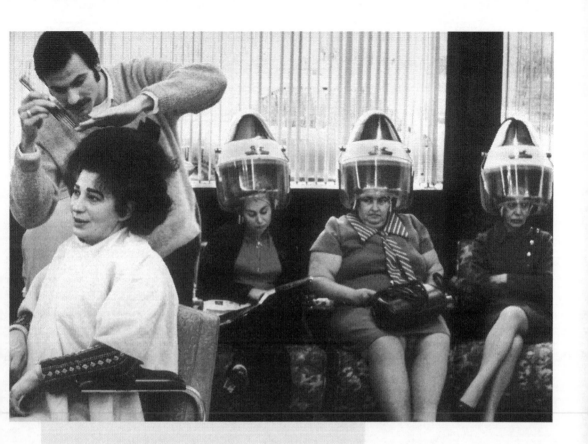

Krishna says that there is no being, either here or in the higher planetary systems, who is free from the influence of the three modes of material nature. Attachment to the body is one of the symptoms of a person so influenced.

to do with material existence. As far as the behavior of transcendentally situated persons, they perform their duties in God consciousness and do not mind whether people honor or dishonor them. Social and political issues are temporary upheavals and disturbances and do not affect them. They can attempt anything for the Lord, but for their personal gain they attempt nothing.

In answer to Arjuna's third question—"How does one transcend the modes of nature?"—the Lord replies, "One who engages in full devotional service, unfailing in all circumstances, at once transcends the modes of material nature and thus comes to the level of impersonal realization [Brahman]. And I am the basis of the impersonal Brahman, which is immortal, imperishable, and eternal and is the constitutional position of ultimate happiness."

The attainment of the Brahman conception of life is the first stage in self-realization. At this stage the Brahman-realized person is transcendental to the material position, but such a person is not actually perfect even in Brahman realization. If one wants, one can gradually rise to the position of realization of Supersoul within and then to the realization of the Supreme Person.

The living entities, although transcendental by nature, desire to enjoy the material world, and due to this desire, they fall under the influence of the three material modes of nature and the illusion of bodily identification. In their constitutional position, living entities are above the three modes of material nature, but they become entangled by association with material nature. Due to this association, the living entities mistakenly think they can dominate and enjoy the material world. But, by engagement in devotional service in full Krishna consciousness, they can be rid of these illusory desires and again be situated in their original, transcendental position.

A chart of the many aspects of the three modes of material nature, as described by Krishna in Chapters 14, 17 and 18 of the *Bhagavad-gita*, appears on pages 150–153.

Although unaware of it, we are revolving in a cycle of repeated birth, death, and rebirth, as though on a ferris wheel, spinning around and around. Sometimes we may be at the top, the human form of life, and then, according to our acts, we may fall to the animal species or lower.

	Ignorance	Passion	Goodness	Pure Goodness*
General Characteristics	Foolishness, madness, illusion, inertia, indolence, and sleep	Unlimited, uncontrollable desires and longings; intense endeavor, greed, bondage to material fruitive activities, and attachment to the fruits of action	Relative purity, illumination, happiness, and freedom from sinful reactions conducive to real knowledge	Complete, unmotivated, unfailing devotion to the Supreme Person; absolute knowledge, purity, illumination, happiness, and freedom from sinful reaction
Destination After Death	The hellish worlds and the animal kingdom	The association of fruitive workers on the earthly planets	The heavenly planets	The eternal abode of the Supreme Lord
Objects of Worship	Ghosts and spirits	Demons, powerful people, and self-proclaimed, imitation gods	The demigods and the impersonal conception of God	The Supreme Lord
Food	Tasteless, stale, putrid, decomposed, unclean; prepared more than three hours before being eaten; remnants of the meals of others; meat, fish, eggs, and liquor	Too bitter, sour, salty, pungent, rich, dry, or hot; causes pain, distress, and disease	Increases longevity, purifies one's existence, gives strength, health, happiness, and satisfaction; nourishing, sweet, juicy, fattening, and palatable; milk products, grains, sugar, fruits, and vegetables	Frees one from past sinful reactions and protects one from future contamination; invokes one's dormant Krishna consciousness; prepared by devotees according to scriptural injunctions and offered with devotion to the Supreme Lord; remnants of the meal of a saintly person
Sacrifice	Performed faithlessly, contrary to scriptural	Performed proudly, ostentatiously, for the	Performed as a duty, according to scriptural regu-	Performed according to scriptural injunctions, and

	injunctions, and with no spiritual food distributed, no hymns chanted, and no remunerations to the priests	sake of some material end or benefit (such as elevation to the heavenly kingdom)	lations, and with no expectation of reward	under the guidance of the spiritual master, to please the Supreme Lord
Austerity	Performed foolishly by means of obstinate self-torture or to destroy or injure others	Performed ostentatiously to gain respect, honor, and reverence; brings only unstable, temporary results	Performed with faith and without desires for one's material benefit *Bodily Austerities:* cleanliness, simplicity, celibacy, nonviolence, offering of respect to the demigods, *brahmanas,* spiritual master, and superiors like the mother and father *Austerities of Speech:* speaking beneficially, truthfully, inoffensively, and with reference to Vedic authorities *Mental Austerities:* serenity, simplicity, gravity, self-control, purity of thought, and detachment from sense gratification	Performed with faith and with a desire to satisfy the Supreme Personality of Godhead
Charity	Performed at an improper time and place, to an unworthy person (like a drunkard) or without respect	Performed to get something in return, with a desire for fruitive results, or in a begrudging mood	Performed as a duty, at the proper time and place, to a worthy person and with no expectation of material returns	Performed only to satisfy the Supreme Lord

	Ignorance	Passion	Goodness	Pure Goodness*
Renunciation	Consists of giving up one's prescribed duties because of illusion	Consists of giving up one's prescribed duties because of fear or because they appear troublesome	Consists of performing one's prescribed duties because they ought to be done and abandoning attachment to the fruits of one's work	Consists of performing one's prescribed duties in Krishna consciousness and employing the fruits of one's work for the satisfaction of Krishna
Knowledge	Very meager; unrelated to the Absolute Truth; breeds attachment to one kind of work as the be-all and end-all; concerned only with bodily comforts, eating, sleeping, mating and defending, and thus resembles the knowledge of animals	Gives rise to speculative doctrines and theories through which one sees the body as the self and consciousness as a temporary by-product of the body; rules out the existence of the eternal, individual soul within	Gives rise to a vision of one undivided spiritual force within the bodies of all living beings (the impersonal conception)	Enables one to see all living beings as eternal, individual, spiritual servants of the supreme living being, Krishna
Action	Irresponsible, violent, distressing to others; performed in illusion, without consideration of scriptural injunctions or future bondage and consequences; results in further foolishness	Performed under false egoism and with great effort, to satisfy one's desires to enjoy the fruits of one's work; results in distress	Performed under scriptural regulations, as a matter of duty, without attachment, and without love and hate, by one who renounces the fruits of one's actions; results in purification	Performed solely for the satisfaction of Krishna and the spiritual master
Worker	Disregards scriptural injunctions	Attached to the fruits	Free from material attach-	Unconditionally serves Krishna and the original

	master under any and all circumstances	ego; enthusiastic, resolute, and unswayed by success or failure	intent upon enjoying them; greedy, envious, unclean; entangled by happiness when successful and distress when unsuccessful	materialistic, obstinate, cheating, lazy, morose, procrastinating, and expert in insulting others
Understanding	Always perfectly considers Krishna through personal realization, confirmed by the scriptures and the spiritual master	Intelligently discriminates, under scriptural direction, between what is to be done and not to be done, what is to be feared and what is not to be feared, and what is liberating and what is binding	Misguided, perverse, and imperfect; cannot distinguish between religion and irreligion, truth and untruth, and what should and should not be done	Considers irreligion to be religion, and religion to be irreligion; strives always in the wrong direction
Determination	Fully engaged in Krishna consciousness and never deviated by anything else	Practically unbreakable; sustained with steadfastness by yoga, which controls the activities of the mind, life, and senses	Fixed upon securing the fruits of religion, economic development, and sense gratification	Cannot go beyond day-dreaming, fearfulness, lamentation, moroseness, and illusion
Happiness	Derived from service rendered by a purified soul to the Supreme Person in an eternal loving relationship; ever-increasing ecstasy; unparalleled by any mundane experience or emotion	Compared to poison in the beginning, but nectar in the end, because it involves control of the mind and senses and awakens one to self-realization	Derived from contact of the senses with their objects; seems like nectar at first, but poison at the end; epitomized by sexual enjoyment	Blind to self-realization; delusion from beginning to end; comes about from sleep, laziness, and illusion

*Pure goodness is fully spiritual and is transcendental to the three modes of material nature.

15

The Yoga of the Supreme Person

T HIS CHAPTER EXPLAINS that the purpose of Vedic study is to understand Krishna. Therefore one who is Krishna conscious, who is engaged in devotional service, has realized the conclusion of the Vedas. The first five verses describe the process of freeing oneself from the attachment to and the possession of matter. The rest of the chapter discusses the highest yoga, the yoga of the Supreme Person.

The Supreme Lord
"It is said that there is an imperishable banyan tree that has its roots upward and its branches downward and whose leaves are the Vedic hymns. One who knows this tree is the knower of the Vedas. The branches of this tree extend downward and upward, nourished by the three modes of material nature. The twigs are the objects of the senses. This tree also has roots going down, and these are bound to the fruitive actions of human society.

Krishna compares the spiritual world to a tree and this material world to the tree's reflection. This world is a replica of the spiritual world, but perverted. What's here is also there, but there it's eternal and real.

God declares that every living entity—in whatever form—is His child, and so He provides life's necessities for all. He is like a cloud that pours rain everywhere, regardless of whether on rock, land, or water.

"The real form of this tree cannot be perceived in this world. No one can understand where it ends, where it begins, or where its foundation is. But with determination one must cut down this strongly rooted tree with the weapon of detachment. Thereafter, one must seek that place from which, having gone, one never returns, and there surrender to that Supreme Person from whom everything began and from whom everything has extended since time immemorial.

"Those who are free from false prestige, illusion, and false association, who understand the eternal, who are done with material lust, who are freed from the dualities of happiness and distress, and who, unbewildered, know how to surrender unto the Supreme Person attain to that eternal kingdom."

For those who are always expecting some honor in this material world, it is not possible to surrender to the Supreme Person. Only when one is free from delusion caused by pride can one begin the process of surrender. Pride is due to illusion, for although people come here, stay for a brief time and then go away, they have the foolish notion that they are the lords of this world. The whole world moves under this impression. People consider the land, this earth, to belong to human society, and they have divided the land under the false impression that they

are the proprietors. Such false conceptions bind them to the material world.

"That supreme abode of Mine is not illumined by the sun or moon, nor by fire or electricity. Those who reach it never return to this material world."

We should be captivated by this information. We should desire to extricate ourselves from this false reflection of reality and transfer ourselves to that eternal world.

"The living entities in this conditioned world are My eternal fragmental parts. Due to conditioned life, they are struggling very hard with the six senses, which include the mind."

As eternal, fragmental parts and parcels of the Supreme Lord, the living entities also have fragmental portions of His qualities, one of which is independence. Every living entity, as an individual soul, has its own personal individuality and minute independence. By misusing that independence, one becomes a conditioned soul dominated by the material modes of nature; by proper use of independence, one is liberated—freed from this material condition of existence and engaged in transcendental loving service to the Lord.

"The living entity in the material world carries different conceptions of life from one body to another as the air carries aromas. Thus the living entity takes one kind of body and again quits it to take another." The living entity itself determines its next body. At the time of death, the consciousness one has created will carry one to the next type of body. One's subtle body, which carries the conception of one's next physical body, develops that body in the next life.

"The living entity, thus taking another gross body, obtains a certain type of ear, eye,

A soul that enters the body of a dog is forced to make the sounds and movements of a dog's body; the dog's body does not allow the soul to act otherwise.

tongue, nose, and sense of touch, which are grouped about the mind. The living entity thus enjoys a particular set of sense objects.

"The foolish cannot understand how a living entity can quit its body, nor can they understand what sort of body it enjoys under the spell of the modes of nature. But one whose eyes are trained in knowledge can see all this." One who is fooled by lust and desire loses all power to understand the stay in a particular body and the ensuing change of body. One who has developed spiritual knowledge, however, can see that the spirit is different from the body, is changing its body, and is enjoying in different ways.

"The splendor of the sun, which dissipates the darkness of this world, comes from Me. And the splendor of the moon and the splendor of fire are also from Me. I enter into each planet, and by My energy they stay in orbit. I become the moon and thereby supply the juice of life to all vegetables. I am the fire of digestion in the bodies of all living entities.

"I am seated in everyone's heart, and from Me come remembrance, knowledge, and forgetfulness. By all the Vedas I am to be known. Indeed I am the compiler of *Vedanta*, and I am the knower of the Vedas." The Supreme Lord is so complete that, for the deliverance of the conditioned souls, He is the supplier and digester of their food, the witness of their activities, the giver of knowledge in the form of the Vedas, and, as the Supreme Person, Lord Krishna, the teacher of the *Bhagavad-gita*.

If a person who is greatly attached to his house dies thinking of it, he may again take birth in the same house, although perhaps not as a human being.

"Those who know Me as the Supreme Lord, without doubting, are the knowers of everything. They therefore engage themselves in full devotional service to Me, O Arjuna. This is the most confidential part of the Vedic scriptures, O sinless one, and I now disclose it. Those who understand this will become wise, and their endeavors will know perfection."

The Lord is like the sun, and ignorance is like darkness. Where the sun is present, there is no question of darkness. Therefore, whenever devotional service is present under the proper guidance of a bona fide spiritual master, there is no question of ignorance.

The sun evaporates ocean water to form a cloud, which then prevents us from seeing the sun. Likewise God creates the illusion which prevents materialists from seeing Him.

16

The Divine and Demonic Natures

IN CHAPTER SIXTEEN THE LORD defines both the transcendental nature with its attendant qualities and the demonic nature with its accompanying qualities. He also explains the advantages of divine qualities and the disadvantages of demonic ones. He begins with the qualities that promote spiritual progress and liberation from the material world.

The Supreme Person

"Fearlessness, purification of one's existence, cultivation of spiritual knowledge, charity, self-control, performance of sacrifice, study of the Vedas, austerity, simplicity, nonviolence, truthfulness, freedom from anger, renunciation, tranquility, aversion to faultfinding, compassion for all, freedom from covetousness, gentleness, modesty, steady determination, vigor, forgiveness, fortitude, cleanliness, and freedom from envy and from the passion for honor—these transcendental qualities, O son of Pandu, belong to godly people endowed with divine nature."

As foam is created by the movements of a wave, atheists believe everything is created from the interaction of physical elements. In this chapter, Krishna describes the behavior of atheists who hold this view.

Right: A story has it that a frog, when informed of the vast ocean beyond his well, began to puff himself up to become as great as that ocean. With each puff he was told that the ocean was still greater than he, until at last, in his final effort, he burst. Similarly, atheists may deny and defy God, but in the end they encounter God as death and lose everything.

Below: Theists see that there is craftsmanship even in a leaf. Such intricacy, they know, has not happened by chance; a magnificent brain conceived its creation.

Left: Chemicals—like citric acid—are produced from life, not vice versa.

"O Arjuna, in this world there are two kinds of created beings. One is called divine and the other demonic. I have already explained to you at length the divine qualities. Now hear from Me of the demonic.

"Pride, arrogance, conceit, anger, harshness, and ignorance—these qualities belong to those of demonic nature, O Arjuna." Ungodly people desire worship and demand respect, although they do not command it. Over trifles they become angry and speak harshly. They do everything whimsically, according to their own desires, and they do not recognize any authority.

"Those who are demonic do not know what is to be done and what is not to be done. Neither cleanliness nor proper behavior nor truth is found in them. They say that this world is unreal, with no foundation, no God in control. They say it is produced of sex desire and has no cause other than lust." The demonic believe matter combined with itself to produce living entities, the soul does not exist, and material nature is the only cause of this world.

"Following such conclusions, the demonic, who are lost to themselves and who have no intelligence, engage in unbeneficial, horrible works meant to destroy the world. Taking shelter of insatiable lust and absorbed in the conceit of pride and false prestige, the demonic, thus illusioned, are always sworn to unclean work, attracted by the impermanent."

The demonic try to enjoy this material world to the utmost limit and therefore always engage in inventing something for their sensory gratification. Such materialistic inventions are considered to reflect advancement of human civilization, but the true result is that people grow increasingly violent and cruel—cruel to animals as well as to other humans. They have no idea how to behave toward one another. Indirectly, Krishna's words anticipate the invention of nuclear weapons, created solely for mass destruction. Due to godlessness such weapons have been invented, as they are not meant for world peace or prosperity.

"The demonic believe that to gratify the senses is the prime necessity of human civilization. Thus until the end of life their anxiety is immeasurable. Bound by a network of hundreds of thousands of desires and absorbed in lust and anger, they secure money by illegal means for sense gratification." The demonic believe that the enjoyment of

Weapons of mass destruction are spawned from the demonic mentality.

*Throughout the world, people with divine
natures and those with demonic natures
reside side by side. In this chapter Krishna
distinguishes them by their qualities.*

the senses is the ultimate goal of life,
and they become more and more
attracted to two things—sex enjoyment and accumulation of material
wealth. And although they are gliding
toward a hellish future, they consider
themselves advanced. They do not
believe in life after death, and they do
not believe that one acquires different
types of bodies according to one's
karma, or activities in this world.

"Thus perplexed by various anxieties and bound by a network of illusions, they become too strongly
attached to sense enjoyment and fall
down into hell."

Demonic people are enamored by
the possessions they already have,
such as land, family, house, and bank
balance, and they are always planning
to improve them. They believe in
their own strength, and they do not
know that their gains are due to
their past good deeds. A competitor of
such demonic persons is their enemy.
There are many demonic people, and

each is an enemy to the others. This enmity becomes deeper and deeper—between persons, then between families, then societies, and at last between nations. Therefore there is constant strife, war, and enmity throughout the world.

Demonic persons may not agree to accept the supremacy of the Lord, and they may act according to their own whims, but their next birth will depend upon the decision of the Supreme Lord rather than upon themselves. By the arrangement of the superior power, the demonic are perpetually put into the wombs of demons, and thus they continue to be envious, full of lust, always violent, hateful, and unclean.

"There are three gates leading to this hell—lust, anger, and greed. Every sane person should give these up, for they lead to the degradation of the soul. The person who has escaped these three gates of hell, O Arjuna, performs acts conducive to self-realization and thus gradually attains the supreme destination.

"Those who discard scriptural injunctions and act according to their own whims attain neither perfection, nor happiness, nor the supreme destination. One should therefore understand what is duty and what is not duty by the regulations of the scriptures. Knowing such rules and regulations, one should act to be gradually elevated." As stated in Chapter Fifteen, all the rules and regulations of the scriptures are intended for knowing Krishna. If we understand Krishna from the *Gita* and become situated in Krishna consciousness, engaging ourselves in devotional service, we have reached the perfection of life.

Behind every arrangement—
large or small—is an arranger.

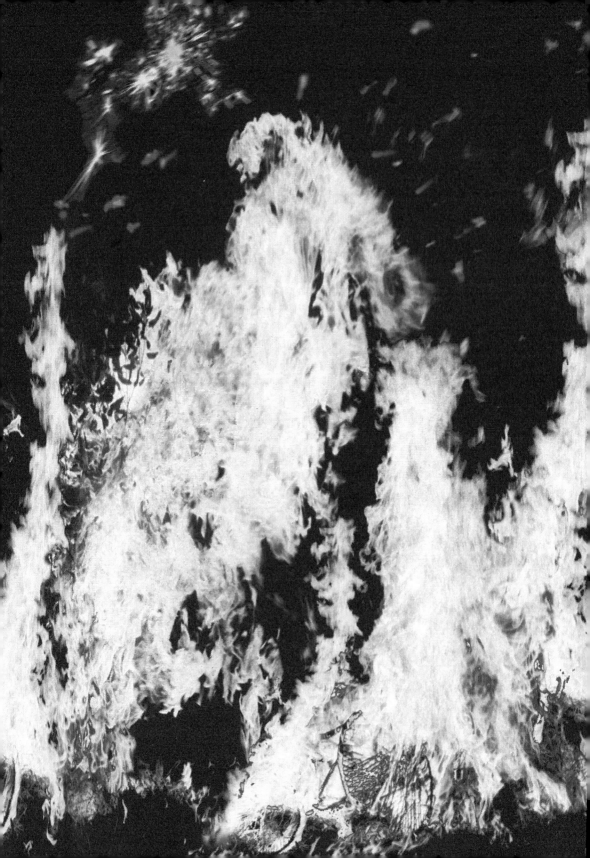

17

The Divisions of Faith

ARJUNA WONDERS ABOUT those who follow rules not mentioned in the scriptures and who have misguided faith in pseudo-gods and gurus.

Arjuna
"O Krishna, what is the situation of those who do not follow the principles of scripture but worship according to their own imaginations? Are they in goodness, in passion, or in ignorance?"

The Supreme Person
"According to the modes of nature acquired by the embodied soul, one's faith can be of three kinds—in goodness, in passion, or in ignorance. Now hear about this.
    "O son of Pandu, according to one's existence under the various modes of nature, one evolves a particular kind

The spirit soul is like a spark coming from a great fire. When the spark falls on dry grass, it easily ignites. Dry grass is likened to the mode of goodness, in which God consciousness readily awakens. When a spark falls on damp ground (which is likened to passion), it may or may not ignite. And if it falls on water (likened to ignorance), it surely will not ignite.

of faith. The living being is said to be of a particular faith according to the modes it has acquired. People in the mode of goodness worship the demigods; those in the mode of passion worship the demons; and those in the mode of ignorance worship the ghosts and spirits.

"Even the food each person prefers is of three kinds, according to the three modes of material nature. The same is true of sacrifices, austerities, and charity. Now hear of the distinctions between them.

"Foods dear to those in the mode of goodness increase the duration of life, purify one's existence, and give strength, health, happiness, and satisfaction. Such foods are juicy, fatty, wholesome, and pleasing to the heart."

Foods that best promote health and increase life's duration, such as milk products, grains, fruits, and vegetables, are dear to those in the mode of goodness. Fatty foods have no connection with animal fat obtained by slaughter. Milk, butter, cheese, and the like give animal fat without the deaths of innocent creatures. Protein is amply available through legumes, whole wheat, other grains, and various food combinations.

"Foods that are too bitter, too sour, salty, hot, pungent, dry, and burning are dear to those in the mode of passion. Such foods cause distress, misery, and disease.

"Food that is tasteless, decomposed and putrid, and food consisting of remnants and untouchable things is dear to those in the mode of darkness.

"Of sacrifices, the sacrifice performed according to the directions of scripture, as a matter of duty, by those who desire no reward, is of the nature of goodness. But sacrifice

By nature's arrangement, carnivorous animals have teeth suited for penetrating and tearing flesh. Human teeth are similar to those of plant-eaters— monkeys, elephants, and cows.

performed for some material benefit, or for the sake of pride, O Arjuna, you should know to be in the mode of passion. Any sacrifice performed without regard for the directions of scripture, without distribution of spiritual food, without chanting of Vedic hymns and remunerations to the priests, and without faith is considered to be in the mode of ignorance."

The Supreme Lord then explains different kinds of austerity, penance, and charity. "Austerity of the body consists in worship of the Supreme Lord, the *brahmanas*, the spiritual master, and superiors like the father and mother, and in cleanliness, simplicity, celibacy, and nonviolence. Austerity of speech consists in speaking words that are truthful, pleasing, beneficial, and not agitating to others, and also in regularly reciting the Vedic literature. And satisfaction, simplicity, gravity, self-control, and purification of one's existence are the austerities of the mind." Austerity for the mind is detachment from sense gratification. When we free our minds from the pursuit of sense enjoyment, only then can we achieve true satisfaction. We should train our minds to think of the welfare of others.

"This threefold austerity, performed with transcendental faith by people not expecting material benefits but engaged only for the sake of the Supreme, is called austerity in goodness.

Penance performed through self-torture and without regard to scriptural guidelines is in the mode of ignorance.

"Penance performed out of pride and for the sake of gaining respect, honor, and worship is said to be in the mode of passion. It is neither stable nor permanent.

"Penance performed out of foolishness, with self-torture or to destroy or injure others, is said to be in the mode of ignorance.

"Charity given out of duty, without expectation of return, at the proper time and place, and to a worthy person is considered to be in the mode of goodness. But charity performed with the expectation of some return, or with a desire for fruitive results, or in a grudging mood, is said to be charity in the mode of passion. And charity performed at an impure place, at an improper time, to unworthy persons, or without proper attention and respect is said to be in the mode of ignorance."

Krishna has explained that penance, sacrifice, charity, and foods are divided into three categories: the modes of goodness, passion, and ignorance. But whether first class, second class, or third class, all these activities and substances are conditioned—contaminated by the material modes of nature.

However, when we direct penance, sacrifice, charity, and foods to the Supreme Lord they become means for spiritual elevation. We should perform all activities for the Supreme Lord, and thus become freed from the influence of material nature.

"Anything done as sacrifice, charity, or penance without faith in the Supreme, O Arjuna, is impermanent. It is called *asat* and is useless both in this life and the next." Krishna consciousness means acting solely for the pleasure

Love of God is already dormant in everyone's heart and simply needs to be evoked. But we are always free to ignore this opportunity, as we are free to avoid the sunshine.

of the Supreme. One who acts directly in Krishna consciousness transcends all three modes of material nature. To achieve this, we must first find the proper spiritual master and learn from that person. Then we can achieve faith in the Supreme. When that faith matures, in due course of time, it is called love of God. This love is the ultimate goal of all living entities.

18

Conclusion ~ The Perfection of Renunciation

As CHAPTER TWO WAS A SYNOPSIS of the *Bhagavad-gita*, so Chapter Eighteen is a summary of all the topics discussed. In this chapter Lord Krishna reveals the purpose of life — to renounce material desires, to attain the transcendental position above the modes of material nature, and to engage in His devotional service.

Arjuna
"O mighty-armed one, I wish to understand the purpose of renunciation and of the renounced order of life."

The Supreme Lord
"The giving up of activities that are based on material desire is what great learned people call the renounced order of life. And giving up the results of all activities is what the wise call renunciation.

If a person uses a stick to strike a snake, that person is responsible for the act, not the stick itself. In the same way, when we fully dedicate ourselves to pleasing the Lord, we become His instruments. The Lord then takes charge in all our acts and frees us from all sins.

"Acts of sacrifice, charity and penance are not to be given up; they must be performed. Indeed, sacrifice, charity and penance purify even the great souls. All these activities should be performed without any attachment or any expectation of result. They should be performed as a matter of duty, O son of Pandu. That is My final opinion."

We should relinquish sacrifices meant for material advancement, as their results are only temporary and fur-

ther bind us to the illusory nature of material life. But sacrifices which purify our existence will elevate us to the spiritual plane. Devotees of the Lord accept any kind of work, sacrifice, or charity that will help them in the discharge of devotional service to the Lord and increase their Krishna consciousness.

"O best of the Pandavas, now hear My judgment about renunciation. The scriptures declare renunciation to be of

When friends and relatives gather at a crematorium, they often reflect, "One day our bodies will also be burnt to ashes. Why are we working so hard? What is the use of it all?" With these thoughts they become renounced, but influenced by material desires born of passion and ignorance, they quickly forget their renunciation.

three kinds. If one gives up one's prescribed duties because of illusion, such renunciation is said to be in the mode of ignorance. Prescribed duties should never be renounced." Work for material satisfaction will not advance us on the spiritual path. But activities such as cooking and offering food to the Supreme Lord, and then eating the remnants of such offerings, inspire us to more spiritual activity and should never be renounced.

"Those who give up prescribed duties as troublesome or out of fear of bodily discomfort have renounced in the mode of passion. Such action never leads to the elevation of renunciation." A Krishna conscious person does not renounce earning money from fear of performing fruitive activities. If by working we can engage our money in the service of God, or if by rising early in the morning we can advance our God consciousness, we must conquer over our mental resistance and feelings of inconvenience.

"O Arjuna, when people perform their prescribed duties only because they ought to be done, and renounce all material association and all attachment to the fruits, their renunciation is in the mode of goodness." The Lord's devotees act without attachment to the results of their activities. They dissociate from the material modes of work. Thus Krishna conscious office workers do not identify with the work of the office, nor with the workers in the office. They simply work for Krishna, and by giving the results of their work to Krishna, they are acting transcendentally.

"It is indeed impossible for an embodied being to give up all activities. But one who renounces the fruits of action is truly renounced. For one who is not renounced, the threefold fruits of action—desirable [heavenly], undesirable [hellish], and mixed—accrue after death. But those who are in the renounced order of life have no such results to suffer or enjoy.

"O mighty-armed Arjuna, according to the *Vedanta* there are five causes for the accomplishment of all action. Now learn of these from Me: the field of action [the body], the performer, the various senses, the many different kinds of endeavor, and ultimately the Supersoul—these are the five factors of action. Whatever right or wrong action a person performs by body, mind, or speech is caused by these five factors. Therefore one who thinks oneself the only doer, not considering the five factors, is certainly not very intelligent and cannot see things as they are.

"Those who are not motivated by false ego, whose intelligence is not entangled, though they kill people in this world, do not kill. Nor are such persons bound by their actions." Anyone who acts in Krishna consciousness under the direction of the Supersoul or the Supreme Person is never affected by reactions, even of killing. When a soldier kills under the command of a superior officer, he is not subject to being judged. But if

A God conscious person sees the hand of the Lord behind everything. Not a blade of grass moves without His will.

In the mode of goodness one may think that at liberation the soul merges into an all-pervasive eternal light. Yet Krishna declares that the soul never loses its individuality. A bird may seem to merge into a tree, but in fact the bird still exists. (Follow the pointer up.)

a soldier kills on his own behalf, then he is accountable and will be judged in a court of law.

Next, the Lord explains knowledge in the three modes of material nature (as described in the charts on pages 150-153). In summary, He says that knowledge concerning the spirit soul which is transcendent to this mortal

body is called knowledge in the mode of goodness; knowledge producing many theories and doctrines by dint of mundane logic and mental speculation is the product of the mode of passion; and knowledge concerned only with keeping the body comfortable is said to be in the mode of ignorance.

He continues to explain work, workers, action, understanding and determination, according to the three modes of material nature (also shown on the chart).

"O best of the Pandavas, now please hear from Me about the three kinds of happiness by which the conditioned souls enjoy, and by which they sometimes come to the end of all distress.

"That which in the beginning may be just like poison but at the end is just like nectar and which awakens one to self-realization is said to be happiness in the mode of goodness." In the pursuit of self-realization, we need to follow many rules and regulations to control the mind and senses and to concentrate the mind on the self. All these procedures are difficult, often even bitter like poison, but if we succeed in following the regulations and attain the transcendental position, we begin to drink real nectar and enjoy life.

"That happiness which is derived from contact of the senses with their objects and which appears like nectar at first but poison at

the end is of the nature of passion. And that happiness which is blind to self-realization, which is delusion from beginning to end and which arises from sleep, laziness, and illusion is of the nature of ignorance.

"There is no being existing, either here or among the demigods in the higher planetary systems, who is free from these three modes of material nature.

"Brahmanas [learned and pious teachers], kshatriyas [military fighters and governmental administrators], vaisyas [farmers and merchants], and sudras [laborers] are distinguished by the qualities born of their own natures in accordance with the material modes, O chastiser of the enemy.

"Peacefulness, self-control, austerity, purity, tolerance, honesty, knowledge, wisdom, and religiousness—these are the natural qualities by which the brahmanas work.

"Heroism, power, determination, resourcefulness, courage in battle, generosity, and leadership are the natural qualities of work for the kshatriyas.

"Farming, cow protection, and business are the natural work for the vaisyas, and for the sudras there is labor as well as service to others.

"By working according to one's nature, everyone can become perfect. Now please hear from Me how this can be done.

The happiness one gets from society, friendship, and love is like a drop of water in the desert. In the vast desert, one drop of water is insignificant. Similarly, material happiness is insignificant. It cannot satisfy one's innermost desire for spiritual pleasure.

"By worship of the Lord, who is the source of all beings and who is all-pervading, people can attain perfection through performing their own work." We should think that we are engaged occupationally by the Supreme Lord, the master of the senses. And with the results of the work in which we are engaged, we should worship the Supreme Lord. In this way the Supreme Lord Himself will take charge of delivering us, and by His mercy we will achieve the highest perfection.

"It is better to engage in one's own occupation, even though one may perform it imperfectly, than to accept another's occupation and perform it perfectly. Duties prescribed according to one's nature are never affected by sinful reactions." We should not imitate another's duty. A person who is by nature attracted to the kind of work done by *sudras* should not artificially claim to be a *brahmana*, although that person may have been born into a *brahmana* family. In this way, one should work according to one's own nature; no work is abominable, if performed in the service of the Supreme Lord. Whether one is a *brahmana*, a *kshatriya*, a *vaisya*, or a *sudra* doesn't matter if one serves the Supreme Lord by one's work. But anything done for personal sense gratification is a cause of bondage. The conclusion is that we all should work according to the particular modes of nature we have

Farmers are enjoined by Krishna to protect cows and bulls, for these gentle animals provide us milk for nourishment and muscle for heavy work.

acquired and should decide to work only to serve the supreme cause of the Supreme Lord.

"Every endeavor is covered by some fault, just as fire is covered by smoke. Therefore you should not give up the work born of your nature, even if such work is full of fault.

"Those who are self-controlled and unattached and who disregard all material enjoyments can obtain, by practice of renunciation, the perfect stage of freedom from reaction."

Renunciation means that we are always thinking of ourselves as parts and parcels of the Supreme Lord, and are

therefore aware that the results of our work belong only to Him. This is God consciousness. With this mentality we are satisfied because we are acting for the Supreme. Thus we become attached to the spiritual; we become accustomed to taking pleasure in the transcendental happiness derived from the service of the Lord.

The devotee in God consciousness laments for nothing nor desires for anything. Since God is full, the living entities who are engaged in His service also become full in themselves. Because pure devotees see everything in relation to God, they are naturally always joyful. They do not

Although full of smoke, fire still does its work of burning. In the same way, though our efforts may be flawed, we can still serve the Supreme Lord by our work.

see persons in the material world as higher or lower than one another; higher and lower positions are ephemeral, and devotees disregard ephemeral appearances and disappearances.

"One can understand Me as I am, as the Supreme Person, only by devotional service. And when one is in full consciousness of Me by such devotion, one can enter into the kingdom of God." If we want to understand the Supreme Lord, we have to undertake pure devotional service under the guidance of a pure devotee. Otherwise, the truth of the Supreme Lord will always be hidden. No one can understand God simply by erudite scholarship or mental speculation. Only one who is actually engaged in Krishna consciousness and devotional service can understand who and what Krishna is. And one who is fully conversant with the science of Krishna becomes eligible to enter into the spiritual kingdom, the eternal, transcendental abode of Krishna.

"Though engaged in all kinds of activities, My pure devotee, under My protection, reaches the eternal and imperishable abode by My grace. In all activities just depend upon Me and work always under My protection. In such devotional service, be fully conscious of Me."

We may argue that Arjuna was acting under the personal instruction of Krishna, but when Krishna does not appear to be present (to those of us who cannot perceive Him at all times), then how should we act? If we act according to the direction of Krishna in the *Bhagavad-gita*, as well as under the guidance of Krishna's bona fide representatives, then the results will be the same. We should

As the fingers naturally serve the body and become vitalized, the soul wants to serve the Supreme Soul and become fulfilled.

have no goal in life except acting in Krishna consciousness just to satisfy Krishna. And while acting in this way, we should think of Krishna only, in the knowledge that we have been appointed by Krishna to discharge these particular duties. While acting in such a way, we naturally have to think of Krishna. This is perfect Krishna consciousness. We cannot, however, act whimsically and then offer the results to the Supreme Lord. That sort of duty is not devotional service to the Lord.

"If you become conscious of Me, you will pass over all the obstacles of conditioned life by My grace. If, however, you do not work in such consciousness but act through false ego, not hearing Me, you will be lost. If you do not act according to My direction and do not fight, then you will be falsely directed. By your nature you will have to be engaged in warfare. Under illusion you are now declining

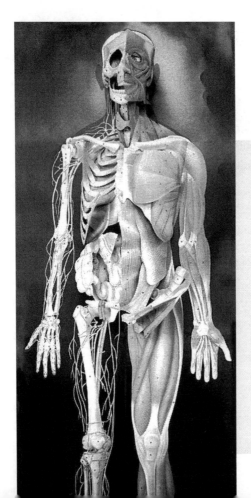

When Krishna spoke the Bhagavad-gita thousands of years ago, He described the body as a machine made of material energy. Today this is confirmed, as bodily organs and limbs—the heart, lungs, legs, and so on—are sometimes replaced by other machines. The machine of the human body is designed by the Lord to enable the living entity to function in this world and, at the same time, become spiritually elevated.

to act according to My direction. But, compelled by the work born of your own nature, you will act all the same, O Arjuna." If we refuse to act under the Supreme Lord's direction, then the modes in which we are situated compel us to act. Everyone is under the spell of changeable combinations of the modes of nature, and is acting accordingly. But those who voluntarily engage themselves under the direction of the Supreme Lord become glorious.

"The Supreme Lord is situated in everyone's heart and is directing the wanderings of all living entities, who are seated as on a machine, made of the material energy. Surrender unto Him utterly. By His grace you will attain transcendental peace and the supreme and eternal abode." The Supreme Lord, as the localized Supersoul, sits in the heart, directing the living being. Upon changing bodies, the living entity forgets its past deeds, but the Supersoul, as the knower of the past, present, and future, remains the witness of all the soul's activities. Therefore, all the activities of a living entity are directed by the Supersoul. The living entity gets what it deserves—the results of its actions—and is carried by the material body, which is created from the material energy under the direction of the Supersoul. As soon as a living entity is placed in a particular type of body, it must work under the spell of that bodily situation. One must, therefore, surrender unto the Supreme Person; that will relieve one from all kinds of miseries of this material existence and, at the end, will enable one to reach the Supreme Lord.

"Thus I have explained to you knowledge still more confidential. Deliberate on this fully, and then do what

you wish to do." God does not interfere with the independence of the living entity. Surrender to the Supreme Lord
is in the best interest of the living entities. Before surrendering, we are free to deliberate on this subject as far as
our intelligence takes us; that is the best way to come to
accept the instruction of the Supreme Lord.

"Because you are My very dear friend, I am speaking to
you My supreme instruction, the most confidential knowledge of all. Hear this from Me, for it is for your benefit.
Always think of Me, become My devotee, worship Me,
and offer your homage unto Me. Thus you will come to
Me without fail. I promise you this because you are My
very dear friend."

This is the essence of the teachings of the Bhagavad-gita.
In the human form of life we have the opportunity and
the free will to mold our lives so that we can always think
of Krishna. This is the most important instruction in all
Vedic literature, the most essential part of knowledge—

meant not only for Arjuna, but for all living entities. Whoever follows the path of Arjuna can become a dear friend to Krishna and obtain the same perfection as Arjuna.

"Abandon all varieties of religion and just surrender unto Me. I shall deliver you from all sinful reactions. Do not fear."

In summarizing the *Bhagavad-gita*, the Lord requests Arjuna to give up all the processes of knowledge and religion that have been explained to him and choose simply to surrender to Krishna. We may think that, unless we are free from all sinful reactions, we cannot surrender to God. Addressing such doubts Krishna states that, even if we are not free from all sinful reactions, simply by surrendering to Him, we are freed automatically. Even through the most herculean efforts, we cannot rid ourselves of our sinful reactions and our entanglement in the cycle of birth and death. We simply must unhesitatingly accept Krishna as

Sometimes the beach is covered by water and, at other times, not. Likewise, the living beings, the Lord's marginal energy, are sometimes covered by His material energy and, at other times, take shelter of the Lord and become free.

the supreme savior of all living entities. With faith and love we should surrender unto Him. We may be perplexed as to how we can give up all forms of religion and simply surrender to Krishna, but such worry is useless.

"O Arjuna, have you heard this with an attentive mind? And are your ignorance and illusions now dispelled?"

Arjuna
"My dear Krishna, O infallible one, my illusion is now gone. I have regained my memory by Your mercy. I am now firm and free from doubt and am prepared to act according to Your instructions."

Bhagavad-gita is the supreme instruction in religion and morality: become a devotee of Krishna and surrender unto Him. As minute parts and parcels of Krishna, the living entities have a tendency to be in contact with either the material energy or the spiritual energy. In other words, the living entities are situated between the two energies of the Lord, and because they belong to the superior energy of the Lord, they have a particle of independence. By proper use of our independence, we can receive the supreme directive of Krishna. Thus we can realize our natural and original state of immortality, knowledge, and transcendental happiness.

Wherever there is Krishna, the master of all mystics, and wherever there is Arjuna, the supreme archer, there will also certainly be opulence, victory, extraordinary power, and morality.

The Author of
Bhagavad-gita As It Is

His Divine Grace A.C. Bhaktivedanta Swami Prabhupada appeared in this world in 1896 in Kolkata, India. He first met his spiritual master, Srila Bhaktisiddhanta Sarasvati Goswami, in Kolkata in 1922. Bhaktisiddhanta Sarasvati, a prominent religious scholar and the founder of sixty-four Gaudiya Mathas (Vedic institutes), liked this educated young man and convinced him to dedicate his life to teaching Vedic knowledge. Prabhupada became his student and in 1933 at Allahabad, became his formally initiated disciple.

At their first meeting, in 1922, Srila Bhaktisiddhanta Sarasvati requested Prabhupada to broadcast Vedic knowledge through the English language. In the years that followed, Prabhupada wrote a commentary on the *Bhagavad-gita,* assisted the Gaudiya Matha in its work and, in 1944, started *Back to Godhead,* an English fortnightly magazine. Maintaining the publication was a struggle. Single-handedly, Prabhupada edited it, typed the manuscripts, checked the galley proofs, and even distributed the individual copies. Once begun, the magazine never stopped; it is now being continued by his disciples in the West and is published in over thirty languages.

Recognizing Prabhupada's philosophical learning and devotion, the Gaudiya Vaishnava Society honored him in 1947 with the title "Bhaktivedanta." In 1950, at the age of fifty-four, Prabhupada retired from married life, adopting the *vanaprastha* (retired) order to devote more time to his studies and writing. Prabhupada traveled to the holy city of Vrindavana, where he lived in humble circumstances in the historic medieval temple of Radha-Damodara. There he engaged for several years in deep study and writing. He accepted the renounced order of life (*sannyasa*) in 1959. At Radha-Damodara, Prabhupada began work on his life's masterpiece: a multivolume annotated translation of the eighteen-thousand-verse *Srimad-Bhagavatam (Bhagavata Purana).* He also wrote *Easy Journey to Other Planets.*

After publishing three volumes of the *Bhagavatam*, Prabhupada came to the United States in September 1965, to fulfill the mission of his spiritual master. Subsequently, Prabhupada wrote more than sixty volumes of authoritative annotated translations and summary studies of the philosophical and religious classics of India.

When he first arrived by freighter in New York City, Prabhupada was practically penniless. Only after almost a year of great difficulty did he establish the International Society for Krishna Consciousness, in July of 1966. Before his passing away on November 14, 1977, he guided the Society and saw it grow to a worldwide confederation of more than one hundred *asramas*, schools, temples, institutes and farm communities.

Prabhupada's most significant contribution, however, is his books. Highly respected by the academic community for their authority, depth and clarity, they are used as standard textbooks in numerous college courses. His writings have been translated into over eighty languages. The Bhaktivedanta Book Trust, established in 1972 to publish Prabhupada's work, has thus become the world's largest publisher of books in the field of Vedic philosophy, religion, literature and culture.

The Photographers for BHAGAVAD-GITA: A PHOTOGRAPHIC ESSAY

YADUBARA DAS AND VISAKHA DEVI DASI, a husband and wife team, met while they were studying photography at Rochester Institute of Technology in New York. In 1971 they traveled to India where they eventually became disciples of Bhaktivedanta Swami Prabhupada. Together they made and continue to make documentary films about Prabhupada and about the philosophy and culture of Krishna consciousness. They have two daughters and are based in Saranagati Village, an off-the-grid community of followers of the *Bhagavad-gita* located in the wilds of British Columbia.

Glossary

Absolute—the ultimate, underlying and all-inclusive reality that depends upon nothing else for its existence. All other things depend upon it.

Absolute Truth—the ultimate source of all energies.

Arjuna—an intimate friend and eternal associate of Lord Krishna. Krishna became his chariot driver and spoke the *Bhagavad-gita* to him.

Astanga-yoga—(asta-eight + anga-part) a mystic yoga system propounded by Patanjali in his Yoga-sutras and consisting of eight parts, which progress from moral practices to deep meditation on God.

Avatar—literally means "one who descends." A partially or fully empowered incarnation of the Lord who descends from the spiritual sky to the material universe with a particular mission described in scriptures.

Banyan tree—a sacred tree of the fig family with self-rooting branches.

Battle of Kurukshetra—a battle between the Kurus and the Pandavas, which took place five thousand years ago and before which Lord Krishna spoke the *Bhagavad-gita* to Arjuna.

Bhagavad-gita—a seven-hundred verse record of a conversation between Lord Krishna and His disciple, Arjuna, from the Bhishma Parva of the Mahabharata of Vedavyasa. Krishna teaches the science of the Absolute Truth and the importance of devotional service to the despondent Arjuna. It summarizes all Vedic knowledge about the soul, God, sanatana-dharma, sacrifice, yoga, karma, reincarnation, the modes of material nature, Vedanta and pure devotion.

Bhagavan—the Supreme Personality of Godhead who possesses in full the opulences of wealth, beauty, strength, knowledge, fame, and renunciation.

Bhakti—devotional service to the Supreme Lord that is untinged by sense gratification or philosophical speculation.

Bhakti-yoga—the system of cultivation of bhakti, or pure devotional service to God.

Brahmajyoti—the impersonal bodily effulgence emanating from the transcendental body of the Supreme Lord Krishna, which constitutes the brilliant illumination of the spiritual sky. For many mystics and philosophers the world over, the brahmajyoti is the indefinable One from which all things emerge in the beginning and merge into at the end.

Brahman—(1) the infinitesimal spiritual individual soul; (2) the impersonal, all-pervasive aspect of the Supreme; (3) the Supreme Personality of Godhead; (4) the mahat-tattva, or total material substance.

Buddha—an incarnation of Krishna and the founder of Buddhism who lived during the 5th century B.C. He appeared to bewilder atheists and dissuade them from performing unnecessary animal sacrifices.

Chaitanya Mahaprabhu—(1486-1534) Lord Krishna in the aspect of His own devotee. He appeared in Navadvipa, West Bengal, and inaugurated the congregational chanting of the holy names of the Lord to teach pure love of God by means of sankirtana.

Consciousness—the irreducible symptom of the self (living entity) that knows, feels and wills. Subtle mind, intelligence and false ego are imposed upon consciousness by the three modes of nature. But though the modes cover it, consciousness remains essentially pure, eternally.

Demigods—universal controllers and residents of the higher planets who assist the Lord in the management of the universe.

Dharma—the occupational eternal duty of the living entity, inseparable from the soul itself.

False ego—the soul's wrong identification with matter.

Hare Krishna mantra—a sixteen-word prayer composed of the names Hare, Krishna, and Rama: Hare Krishna, Hare Krishna, Krishna Krishna, Hare Hare, Hare Rama, Hare Rama, Rama Rama, Hare Hare. The chanting of this mantra is the most recommended means for spiritual progress in this age, as it enables one to transcend the temporary designations of race, religion, and nationality and to understand one's true identity as an eternal spiritual being.

Hinduism—a word derived from Sindhu, the name of a river in present-day Pakistan. Beginning around 1000 AD, invading armies from the Middle East called the place beyond the Sindhu river Hindustan and the people who lived there the Hindus. (Due to the invaders' language, the s was changed to h.) In the centuries that followed, the term Hindu became accepted even to the Indians themselves as a general name for their religious traditions. The word Hindu, however, is not found in the Vedic scriptures upon which these traditions are based.

Japa—the soft recitation of Krishna's holy names.

Jivatma—the living entity, who is an eternal soul, individual but part and parcel of the Supreme Lord.

Kali-yuga—the present age in which we are now living, which is characterized by irreligious practices, quarrel and stringent material miseries.

Karma—1. material action performed according to scriptural regulations; 2. action pertaining to the development of the material body; 3. any material action which will incur a subsequent reaction; 4. the material reaction one incurs due to fruitive activities. This Sanskrit word means 'action' or, more specifically, any material action that brings a reaction binding us to the material world. According to the law of karma, if we cause pain and suffering to other living beings, we must endure pain and suffering in return.

Kirtan—the devotional process of chanting the names and glories of the Supreme Lord.

Krishna—literally, the all-attractive Lord. The main Sanskrit name of the original Supreme Personality of Godhead. Lord Krishna is the source of all incarnations, and no one is equal to Him or greater than Him. He is Bhagavan, the possessor of six opulences in unlimited fullness.

Mantra—(man-mind + tra-deliverance) a spiritual sound vibration that delivers the mind from its material inclinations and illusion.

Maya—an energy of Krishna's which deludes the living entity into forgetfulness of Him.

Omkara—the transcendental sound *om*, which symbolically denotes the Personality of Godhead as the root of the creation, maintenance and destruction of the cosmic manifestation.

Paramatma—the Supersoul, the localized aspect of the Supreme Lord residing in the heart of each embodied living entity and pervading all of material nature.

Personalism—the philosophical position that accepts personality as ultimate.

Prasada (or prasadam)—literally means mercy and usually refers to food prepared for the pleasure of Krishna and offered to Him with love and devotion. Because Krishna tastes the offering, the food becomes spiritualized and purifies anyone who eats it.

Rama—the Absolute Truth who is the source of unlimited pleasure.

Sanatana-dharma—literally, the "eternal activity of the soul," or the eternal religion of the living being, namely to render service to God.

Sankirtan—the sacrifice prescribed for this age, namely the congregational chanting of the name, fame and pastimes of the Supreme Lord.

Siva—the superintendent of the mode of ignorance who takes charge of destroying the universe at the time of annihilation.

Soul—the eternal living entity who is part and parcel of the Supreme Lord and is known in Sanskrit as jiva, jiva-atma or atma. The symptom of the soul is consciousness.

Supersoul—known as Paramatma in Sanskrit, the localized expansion of the Supreme Lord residing in the heart of each embodied living entity and pervading all of material nature. The Supersoul dwells within the hearts of all living beings next to the soul and from Him come the living entity's knowledge, rememberance and forgetfulness.

Swami—one fully in control of his senses and mind; the title of one in the renounced, or sannyasa, order.

Vaishnavism—the science of bhakti-yoga to Vishnu or Krishna.

Vedas—literally, knowledge; the message of the transcendental realm that has come down to this phenomenal world through sound. The system of eternal wisdom for the gradual upliftment of all mankind from the state of bondage to the state of liberation.

Vedic—pertaining to a culture in which all aspects of human life are under the guidance of the Vedas.

Vrindavana—Krishna's eternal abode where He fully manifests His quality of sweetness.

Yoga—literally, connection; the discipline of self-realization meant for linking one's consciousness with God. According to the *Bhagavad-gita*, the most sublime form of yoga is bhakti-yoga, the yoga of pure devotion to God.

THE MOST BEAUTIFUL THING IN THIS WORLD
IS THE BHAGAVAD-GITA
BECAUSE THEREIN KNOWLEDGE IS IMPARTED BY
THE PERSONALITY OF GODHEAD
HIMSELF.

His Divine Grace
A. C. Bhaktivedanta Swami Prabhupada

95634310R00135

Made in the USA
Middletown, DE
27 October 2018